Carlo Middione's

TRADITIONAL
PASTA

Carlo Middione's

TRADITIONAL
PASTA

Carlo Middione

Color Illustrations by Linda Hillel and Roger Yepsen

TEN SPEED PRESS
BERKELEY, CALIFORNIA

A Kirsty Melville Book

Ten Speed Press
Box 7123
Berkeley, California 94707

Distributed in Australia by E.J. Dwyer Pty. Ltd., in Canada by Publishers Group West, in New Zealand by Tandem Press, in South Africa by Real Books, and in the United Kingdom and Europe by Airlift Books.

Cover and text design by Big Fish Books, San Francisco.
Line drawings on pages 19, 95, 97 by Akiko Shurtleff.
Plates and bowls on pages 30, 42 (far left), and 92 courtesy of Biordi Art Imports, San Francisco.

Library of Congress Cataloging-in-Publication Data
Middione, Carlo.
    Carlo Middione's traditional pasta/Carlo Middione.—1st Ten Speed ed.
            p.cm.
            Rev. ed. of: Pasta! Cooking it, loving it. 1982
            Includes index
            ISBN 0-89815-805-2
            1. Cookery (pasta) I. Middione, Carlo. Pasta! Cooking it, loving it. II. Title
    TX809.M17M5297 1996
641.8'22—dc20   95-50757
First Ten Speed Press printing, 1996   CIP

Printed in Hong Kong

1 2 3 4 5 6 7 8 9 10 — 00 99 98 97 96

[CONTENTS]

[ACKNOWLEDGMENTS]

This update of my book by Ten Speed Press, might never have occurred if not for the sharp eyes and fine-tuned ears of Cynthia Traina on a chance encounter, and her swift action and willingness to see it happen. Thank you, Cynthia.

Kirsty Melville, publisher of Ten Speed Press, gets a big thanks for moving fast, being agreeable, and letting serendipity have some space in this book, along with a little nature. She is smart and thoughtful and likes happy authors.

Of course, I thank and applaud Doe Coover, my agent who is ever hovering, cajoling, encouraging, interceding, promoting, and yet, never yelling—how remarkable.

I also thank Vivande's chef de cuisine, Kevin C. Baker, for working so hard and maintaining the integrity of our dishes while pushing our horizons; I thank John Zhao, Vivande's sous chef, who is faster than anyone alive, dedicated, and has infallible taste.

Lorena Jones, my editor, must take bows for letting me have a beautiful book of which I am proud, and for encouraging me to do better work (and a lot of it).

I thank Annamaria Gasperini for her invaluable help in translating the devilish Italian grammer into English.

And, yet again, I thank my beautiful wife, Lisa, for always supporting and encouraging me, and for giving my life great meaning. My original acknowledgments follow, and they still hold true.

After years of believing I had to work at things I didn't enjoy to make a living, I am forever indebted to those who have recognized my teaching and sharing of the Italian cooking I love to do. Specifically, I am thankful for the encouragement and support of Mary Risley, Tante Marie's Cooking School; Ron Batori, Daniele Carlyle, and Silvio D. Plaz, California Culinary Academy; Nancy Fleming, Jack Hansen, and the producers of "A.M. San Francisco"; Harvey Steiman, Margaret Mallory, Jana Allen, and others who have so kindly critiqued my work in the press; my colleagues, my students, and the others too numerous to list. It is your response that makes it possible for me to engage in my work as a chef.

I am grateful to my family for giving me a heritage of Italian food culture and a legacy of good cooking; to Irena Chalmers for asking me to write this book about a part of that heritage; and especially to my wife, Lisa, without whose unfailing help, this book, as well as many other projects, could not have been undertaken.

I thank Harper and Row for re-issuing the book in hardback after it was first published in paperback by Irena Chalmers.

I HAVE BEEN given a chance to breathe new life into this book on a subject that typifies so much of my existence—the making, cooking, and eating of pasta! The book, as I first wrote it years ago, still rings true. In some parts I have improved what I wrote about technique or style. In others I have added insights or tips to make the preparation and eating of pasta more useful and, I hope, more enjoyable. Most of it, I simply left alone.

For more than a decade and a half this book, under another name, has been a mainstay in my own kitchen and in the kitchens and libraries of tens of thousands of people. I am pleased and proud that this discourse on pasta has lasted so many years. There is no question these pages have given wisdom, knowledge, direction, and courage to would-be pasta experts and have helped mold them into the real thing. I still get letters telling me so. I am delighted to be able to add some new pasta dishes, some that have become modern classics, to the this edition. Several of these new dishes are from Vivande Porta Via and Vivande Ristorante, my two food arenas, where no
matter what else is served, pasta leads the way.

In updating this book, I was amazed to realize the number of changes that have taken place in the last few years. In the old book I urged people to use "good" olive oil, barely daring to speak of extra virgin, and stated that Prosciutto di Parma could not be legally imported into the United States, which was then an unhappy fact. Now we have dozens of kinds and brands of extra virgin olive oils to choose from, and who hasn't gorged on the absolutely velvety, delicious

Prosciutto di Parma? I can hardly cook without it. Of course, there are loads of different Italian dry pastas to choose from, and an avalanche of cheeses of every type. Another welcome change is that more and more people realize the importance of pasta as a first dish or main dish in the meal. And (this really floors me), many Americans have come to realize that pasta has unique merits that make it delicious on its own. Consequently, I do believe I see a little bit of improvement in the amount of sauce Americans prefer on pasta. Most have gone from wanting their pasta swimming to merely wetted down well—to me, that is encouraging.

For many Americans pasta has become a staple, a "must-have" kind of food. Some people eat it because of implied health benefits, some because it is inexpensive, some because they simply cannot live without its tasty, earthy flavor, and, if correctly cooked, its texture. The increase in the consumption of pasta has led to a heightened interest in sauces and methods of using pasta in meals. Because of pasta's incredible versatility, one can see that there are endless ways to savor it as a major element in the daily diet.

Me, I *never* tire of pasta. I have tired of eating chocolate bars, meat, and fish, but I say proudly and truthfully I have never tired of pasta, whether I eat it or cook it or serve it. It is my hope that this book, now refined a bit and a touch more helpful than it was previously, will stir up interest in the fun of making and eating pasta so that thousands more will cherish its rewards.

Pasta is not simply flour and water or eggs. It is a way of life. Pasta knows no social, political, or economical barriers or influences. It is a godsend for the poor, and the richest of the rich have enjoyed pastas with equal gusto. Pasta may well be the most democratic food in the world, because it does the most good for the most people.

The consideration of pasta resembles a sociological study. There are ape-watchers, bug-watchers, and UFO-watchers; and there are pasta-watchers, of whom I am one. Thousands before me have written about pasta and, undoubtedly, thousands more will do so after me. Too much, or enough, can never be said on the subject. Perhaps the most wonderful thing about pasta is that nobody and everybody is an expert, and pasta is such an indigenous expression in Italy that there can't be any hard-and-fast rules. If you become too didactic about it, you can end up feuding with your friends and neighbors. For safety's sake, the study of pasta must be approached with a keen sense of adventure and an open mind.

In tracing the origins of pasta there are, of course, a few givens. We know that our primitive ancestors first gathered wild wheat, discovered how to hull and cook the grain, and learned to mix it with water to make an edible paste. This grain paste was a staple of most prehistoric civilizations, and it has remained a staple in some form ever since.

Relics from the Etruscan civilization of the fourth century B.C. show that these people had developed the tools to mix flour into dough, roll it out on a table, and cut it into strips. The Latin word *nodellus*, meaning the little knot that pasta can get into if you're not careful to see that the dough isn't sticky, gave us the word "noodles." Other civilizations arrived at the same result using buckwheat, rice, soybeans, mung beans, and other grains and flours.

However, over the centuries, the role of wheat pasta as a significant culinary medium has realized its highest potential in Italy. Nowhere else does pasta show up in so many guises or has it become such a mainstay and a dietary staple as among contemporary Italians, and nowhere else has it achieved cultural expression as an indigenous form of art. Here the pristine and simple flavors of *pastasciutta* (any pasta served with sauce), with butter, and cheese are at one end of the scale, as they are at one end of the country, the north. The complex flavors of the delicious and earthy *Pasta al Forno* (baked pasta) of Sicily in the south represent the other extreme in a very broad range of applications. The pasta dish can take a primary or a secondary place in an Italian meal. Pasta can be very kind to you as a cook when you want to make a particular dish, or you can just see what you have on hand, and pasta will say, "Let's get with it!"

It is said that you can eat pasta every day of the year in Italy without repeating a single dish, and the chances are that many people do exactly that. It is estimated that 80 percent of all southern Italians eat pasta daily and some twice a day, having a *pastasciutta* (with sauce) for lunch and a *pasta in brodo* (in broth) or a *minestra* (in thick soup) for dinner or supper. Italian cooking, after all, is essentially home cooking based on available ingredients, and since pasta comes in a multitude of shapes and sizes, it is not difficult to see how this is possible.

On repeated occasions throughout the centuries, some reactionary Italians have expounded different theories denouncing the overuse of pasta or even claiming it was "evil" food, not to be trusted as nourishment. Public campaigns have even been instituted against the consumption of excessive quantities of macaroni. Some "authorities" have tried to tell the Italian people that pasta was no food for fighters, for virility, or for those who didn't want to get fat. However, the Italians, especially those in the south, have gone right on eating it every day. Their passion for *pastasciutta* is too deeply rooted in taste and custom. Also, a widely diffused superstition prevails that "macaroni," a word today synonymous with all forms of pasta, is said to be derived from the ancient Greek word *makar,* meaning "divinely holy or blessed," and is the antidote to all ills, the universal panacea.

It does seem, though, that these southern Italians know something that we don't know. Recent medical studies have reported a lower incidence of heart disease and cancer among those who eat pasta daily. A comparable study of an Italian-American "ghetto" community whose members followed a diet high in pasta and wine showed virtually no incidence of heart disease below the age of 40 and after that age an incidence of 25 percent of the rate of occurrence among the general United States population.

It is certainly true that one sees far fewer examples of obesity in pasta-eating Italy than in the United States, where we seem to get heavier and heavier with each national survey. However, with the "fitness revolution" of the 1980s and now the "fitness frenzy" and badge-toting fat and exercise police of the 1990s, American media are beginning to pay increasing attention to the integral role of diet and nutrition in health and exercise programs, and to the benefits of reducing cholesterol consumption by eating more poultry and fish and less red meat and saturated fat. Nutritionists stress the importance of complex carbohydrates, especially in unrefined forms, as focal elements in a healthful diet, because they give muscle tissue plenty of food to grow on and far less fat to worry about. An interesting scientific theory published some time ago reminds us that food is the usual reward for all animals, including humans, and that appetite and feeding signals are rooted in the wiring of the central nervous system. Our appetites seem to be signaling some betrayal of satisfaction from the red meat and processed foods we are feeding ourselves. The reason may be that such food fails to satisfy us until we have taken it in excessive amounts, which may well have something to do with our excess weight. The foods we currently eat are relatively new to us in evolutionary terms, because our species originally evolved on a diet of grains and fruit. Calorie for calorie, laboratory evidence shows complex carbohydrate foods are more satisfying to humans; consequently, a greater dietary emphasis on them could well solve both our appetite and excess weight problems.

Personally, I would almost always rather eat a normal serving of good pasta than a steak. I get more immediate satisfaction from the pasta, along with fewer calories and more peace of mind and stomach, than I possibly could get from the meat. Whether made from the whole grain, or refined and enriched with fortified vitamins, the wheat flour in pasta provides a good distribution of essential amino acids to help provide protein, B vitamins (thiamine, riboflavin, and niacin) and iron. The food values are even greater in fresh egg pasta, which is considered to be one of the world's most perfect foods, because it contains virtually all of the essential nutrients.

Pasta is low in fat and sodium and, if properly prepared and served, easily digested. It is an extraordinarily economical source of excellent nutrition, which can be appropriately dressed up or dressed down for almost any eating occasion.

In addition to all these paramount virtues, Italian pasta is an artistic medium, one in which all cooks, would-be cooks, and just plain eaters can find creative expression—and even humor and fun. Imaginative shapes and forms of pasta dressed in inspired sauces bring brilliant colors to the table to delight the soul and the psyche as well as the palate. When something that's good for us is so attractive and easy to take, why don't we use more of it?

Pasta is taken seriously in Italy. Per capita consumption ranges close to 65 pounds per year. In America, the last count I know of is about 20 pounds per person per year, although it is increasing. If Americans could learn what good pasta is, as it is prepared and served in Italy, the rate of consumption in America could grow even more rapidly. Such knowledge would lead to the demand for better-quality pasta in stores and restaurants, and an effort to make it properly at home.

At the risk of insulting some people, I must say that I have always been upset and offended by the way Americans often use pasta merely as an excuse for eating quarts of sauce. This only supports the myth that pasta is fattening, as most sauces surely are when consumed in excess. Also, although Italians are big bread eaters, they never "double up" on wheat products at the same meal.

As a Sicilian-American, I speak from experience. I come from a long line of innkeepers. When my parents came to this country, my father—an accomplished pastry chef—first operated a cafe and bakery in Buffalo, New York, and later a fine dinner house and catering business in Glendale, California. My mother did the general cooking, helped by my aunts and cousins. I grew up in that kitchen and got all my practical training there.

So it saddens me that one of the first and best English-language cookbooks on Italian pasta titles its chapters, "Seafood with Pasta," "Meats with Pasta," "Poultry and Game with Pasta," "Vegetables with Pasta," and even "Leftovers and Pasta." The Italian approach to pasta appears to be lost in this categorical translation, as in Italy the pasta never loses its integrity or is subordinate to any sauce or accompaniment. An important standard of all good Italian cooking is to keep each ingredient unmistakably separate and to preserve each item's special characteristics rather than blending, masking, or disguising it, or covering up textures, tastes, or even blemishes. Things have to be inherently good, without aid, to be successfully presented in an exposed and naked state. The excellence of Italian dishes depends on the excellence of the things that go into them. In the case of pasta dishes, the pasta itself is no exception to this rule. Even the popular and world-famous *Fettuccine all'Alfredo* as served in the restaurants in Rome does not come to the table swimming in sauce (even though most of us *would* like to drink this ambrosia or eat it with a spoon). The pasta is beautifully coated with just the right amount of flavorful sauce. There's no question that it's pasta that you're eating, and it is just as good in and of itself as it ought to be.

Another practice that offends me is the American

habit of overcooking all noodles, including pasta, in almost every one of its forms. If you want your pasta to be maximally digestible and to provide the greatest nutritional benefits, it must be cooked and eaten al dente (literally, "to the teeth," or chewy), that is, firm yet tender. Only this way will it be properly chewed, which is essential to the digestive processes. Mushy and over-cooked, the pasta descends to the stomach as an unmasticated solid mass, where it is quite indigestible.

Lastly, Americans must learn to eat their pasta in the approved Italian manner. If you ask for a spoon for your pasta when eating in Italy, you will be taken as an unappreciative boor and probably be effectively denied admission to the inner sanctum, where Italy's most precious culinary treasures are shared. Use a fork in your right hand only. (You may use it in your left hand, as a concession, if that is natural for you.) Point it downwards and twirl it in the pasta until a reasonable amount is entwined on the fork. Now, lift the fork to your mouth and gently but firmly slurp up the ends of the pasta hanging from it. History tells us that Italians used forks in the sixteenth century, much earlier than anyone else in the rest of Europe. It's anyone's guess how they ate their pasta before then, but, actually, spaghetti street vendors in the south of Italy sold their pasta out of large serving dishes, from which buyers without forks grasped the strands with their thumbs and forefingers, held them high overhead, and lowered them into their wide-open mouths. I am told this was commonplace even as late as the end of the nineteenth century, and such Neapolitan street scenes were visually recorded in drawings by Vuillier and glass-negative photos by Studio Alinari. In Italy's Spaghetti Historical Museum, at Pontedassio, near Genoa, none less than Sophia Loren's advice on spaghetti-eating etiquette is posted thus: "Spaghetti can be eaten successfully if you inhale it like a vacuum cleaner."

While dining in a Roman restaurant, I remember being impressed by an elegant *baronessa,* in a low-cut blue dress, who complained just before dinner, *"Mi sento un po' male"* (I feel a little poorly). She then restored her body and soul before my very eyes by eating a dish of spaghetti. When the spaghetti was set before her, she very matter-of-factly picked up her fork and plunged it into the center of the mass. She spun the fork once and then lifted it, filled with pasta, into her mouth, leaving a trail of spaghetti from her lips to the plate. From there she proceeded literally to inhale, with the most exquisite sounds of sheer appreciation I've ever heard. The strands of pasta disappeared into her mouth without a trace of splatter. By continuous repetition of this process, the *baronessa* polished off the entire plate of pasta and, visibly improved in both appearance and mood, became even more charming than before. After this modest beginning, she was sufficiently revivified to order and consume a *Bistecca alla Fiorentina* (a delicately flavored, yet prodigious Florentine-style steak) and a lovely selection of fresh fruit and assorted cheeses, all moistened and perfumed by some delightful young Frascati white wine. If there ever was an Italian Connection, this was it.

Somewhere my wife found a funny sticker which she posted in our kitchen at home above the range, where it's stayed ever since. It reads, "If you're not Italian, fake it!" If you want to get the most out of your pasta experience, "Fake it till you make it" may not be such bad advice for you to follow.

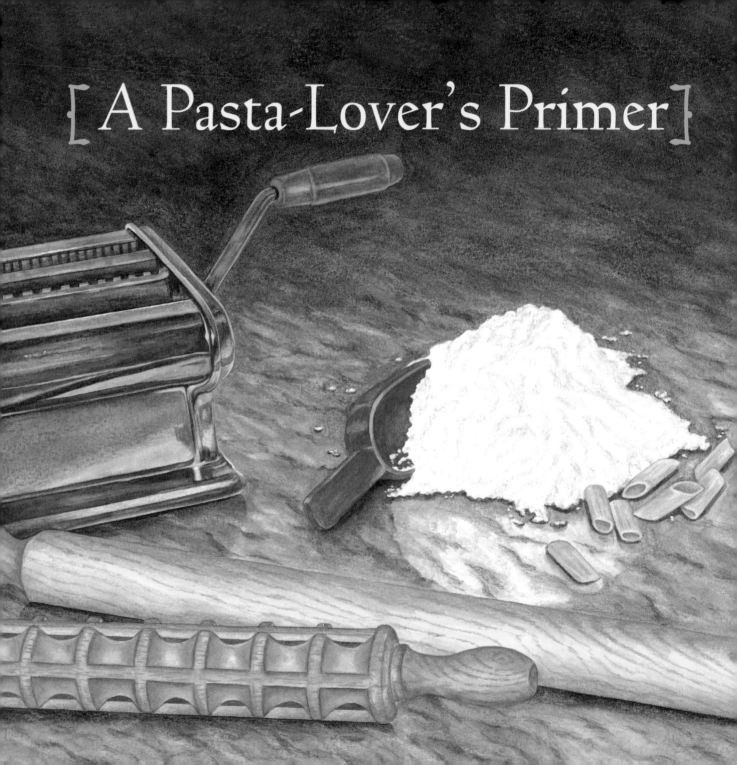

Making, Identifying, and Cooking Pasta (Fare, Conoscere e Come Cucinare La Pasta)

A dish of pasta is only as good as the pasta itself.
—Luigi Barzini, author of *The Italians*

THE HISTORY OF Italian pasta goes back farther than most people realize. It certainly predates Marco Polo by a long shot. There is evidence that the Etruscans, who preceded the Romans, already had pasta pretty much as we know it. Farther south, Arabs occupied Sicily for nearly 400 years. In the twelfth century, they described a concoction called *itriya*, from their word meaning "string," which we know as pasta and was the same as it is made today. Spaghetti in Italian means "little strings." You can see the connection. All over Sicily pasta became known as *tria*. Even now in my cousin's hometown, the old-timers still call spaghetti *trii*. From these tenuous origins, Italians learned to make many pastas by hand, but mostly strings, tubes, and ribbons. Eventually, pasta became a huge industry, feeding masses of Italians since the mid-nineteenth century. Now, Italian pasta exportation is worldwide, and the consumption of pasta continues to grow.

Along the way, pasta-makers discovered that hard durum winter wheat flour, rich in gluten, is stronger and superior to ordinary flour for making pasta. They learned that dough made with this flour does not fall apart in boiling water, and is sturdy enough to hold up when formed into a variety of fanciful shapes. Durum wheat is a rich golden yellow with an almost nutlike flavor and a natural spicy fragrance that is sometimes likened to cinnamon. Durum wheat is then milled into *semola* or flour from which the pasta is made. *Semolina* or *semolino* is merely a coarser, more granular form of this durum flour, which consists almost entirely of the nutritious endosperm particles of the grain.

In Italy, durum flour may be purchased in the stores in a series of different grinds, from coarse to fine. Only a person with bionic arms would ever attempt to make pasta entirely by hand from semolina, the coarsest granules. In America, fine-ground durum is not generally available in consumer markets, as it is too hard for most hand work. Most of the available durum flour is used in industrial pasta production. However, domestic and Italian imported durum semolina (also the categorical name of the product) is increasingly available in retail stores here, and one often hears it touted these days as an essential ingredient in authentic Italian pasta. Nevertheless, I've received many emergency phone calls from cooking school students who were unable to get their pasta dough to come together with the coarse-ground semolina. I've come to the conclusion there may have been some slippage in the translation and usage of *semola* (flour) and *semolina* (grits). Another possibility is that semolina is being offered in the United States today mainly for use in electric home pasta machines. At least *they* may be strong enough to work with it.

After much searching, I have found very good fancy durum flour with which to make pasta, but I have to buy enormous quantities of it. At one point, years ago, I had to have it specially milled for me and the minimum order then was 1,000 pounds. Fancy durum *flour* (that is the operative word) is essentially semolina that is milled as fine as all-purpose flour. It is yellow, very beautiful to look at and silky to the touch. My standard recipe at both my Vivande restaurants is 50 percent semolina and 50 percent fancy durum flour. For 1 pound of mixed flours I use about 4 eggs, but the ratio varies enormously according to the weather, the moisture in the wheat, the moisture in the eggs and their yield, and of course the hand that makes the pasta. This combination of flours makes excellent pasta when using a machine, even a small tabletop, manual roller type. To mix and roll such a pasta totally by hand would be a taxing job, indeed.

For centuries in Italy, pasta has primarily been made in factories located in sunnier coastal areas with favorable drying conditions. Until the introduction of a continuously operated mechanical process in 1939, the work of pasta-making was organized in stages: first, mixing the flour with water or sometimes egg; next, kneading the dough; next, rolling it; and finally, cutting it. From the time of the Renaissance, the Italian pasta-making industry has been carefully controlled under increasingly rigid standards, first by guilds, then by educa-

tional institutions, now by the national government. Today, the law requires that dried commercial Italian pastas be made only with pure durum wheat flour and water, without any artificial colorings or preservatives. To produce colored pasta, only natural vegetables may be added. Dried commercial Italian egg pastas must, by law, contain at least 5 whole eggs for every 2 pounds of flour. In America, where commercial pasta is also made from durum wheat, the flour tends to undergo more processing in the milling stage and thereafter is enriched with fortified vitamins. American commercial egg pastas are generally made with frozen eggs or egg solids, and colored pastas are usually made with powdered dehydrated vegetables or simply vegetable-based dyes.

Handmade or partially handmade fresh *pasta casalinga* (homemade pasta) is still used widely in Italy. Despite the high quality of Italian commercial dried pasta today, there are many who still believe that eating *pasta fresca, fatt' a mano* (fresh pasta, made by hand) is the only way to enjoy the true pasta experience. For sure, both types have their place in the pasta diet, as we shall see later in looking at the recipes. Dough formulas for fresh pasta differ from region to region in Italy. A fine grind of flour, often the product of blending hard wheat with some of a softer type in order to facilitate handwork, may be mixed with whole egg; with egg yolk only for a firm yellow egg pasta; with whole egg and a little water; or with whole egg and a bit of oil. The custom of adding the oil comes from Florence, and it does make the dough easier to work. However, the majority of Italians from the other regions believe that oil makes the pasta too heavy; they would rather spend the extra effort necessary to obtain the desired result. Whole eggs are tenderizers. Sometimes the addition of a little extra egg in proportion to the flour can help out the home pasta-maker who is having difficulty working by hand. Here is the basic formula I use for good results in the United States: *1 pound all-purpose flour and 4 large U.S. Grade A eggs, which yields 1 1/2 pounds of fresh pasta.* Alternatively, the following formula works very well.

MY BASIC FRESH PASTA DOUGH FORMULA

1. Use an all-purpose *unbleached* flour for a well-balanced blend of hard and soft wheat flours. It will give you a sufficiently strong pasta that you will still be able to work by hand.

2. Use ³/₄ cup of flour to 1 large whole egg at room temperature. Because flour varies with the humidity in the climate, the altitude, and other factors, and because eggs vary in size and in the way the hens that lay them have been fed, this proportion is only approximate and subject to adjustment when you have gained a feel for the optimal consistency of the dough.

3. In the kitchen we describe a batch of pasta by the number of eggs in it; that is, we make a 1-egg pasta, a 2-egg pasta, a 3-egg pasta, and so on by simply increasing the flour proportionately.

4. The 1-egg pasta will yield about ¹/₂ pound of fresh pasta. This will feed one person a generous main-dish serving and possibly two persons a first-course pasta. While 2 ounces of commercial dried pasta are used for a first-course serving per person, remember than fresh pasta is wetter and heavier than the dried.

5. In general, a 3-egg pasta is about the most you will be able to make entirely by hand. Pasta-making takes a good bit of strength. For larger batches, you will probably need the aid of one or more machines. Even then you still may have to subdivide the batch into smaller quantities in order to work it properly.

MAKING THE DOUGH

The making of pasta by hand is an art, not a science. You must make a lot of it all the time and practice constantly or you will have inconsistency in your results. It is like playing the piano or the violin or, as I have been told, sex. If you don't use it, you lose it.

By Hand

Heap the flour on a wooden or other cool surface and make a well in the center. Add the egg and immediately start to "scramble" the egg into the flour in a circular motion with a fork. Keep pushing bits of flour into the egg. When the mixture is holding together well and looks as if you can work it with your hands, do so. Knead the mass for about 6 or 7 minutes to incorporate as much flour into it as possible. It will be very stiff and hard to work, but do it anyway. Rest frequently as needed. When properly kneaded, the dough will have a shiny look to it. Wrap it well in plastic or waxed paper and let it rest for about 20 to 30 minutes on the table. *Do not refrigerate it!*

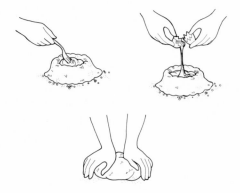

The kneading process is essential to good pasta dough, as it develops the natural elasticity of the flour's gluten, which is a complex combination of proteins. Knead with the heal of your hand by pushing down and away from you, turning the dough a quarter turn, and repeating. Proper kneading should leave the dough smooth and silky. When the dough is well kneaded, the gluten is so elastic that it would shrink up if you tried to roll it out immediately. Cover the dough in plastic wrap and let rest once again. While the dough rests, the gluten relaxes, which enables it to be rolled. (Be sure to remove the wrap when ready to roll.)

By Food Processor

Place the flour in the bowl. Start the blade moving and drop in the egg. Process until the mixture looks like grains of sand. Stop the machine, lift off the lid; take some of the mixture and squeeze it between your thumb and fingers. If it adheres to itself and forms what appears to be the beginning of a dough, empty the contents of the processor onto a board, press together with your hands, knead, and let the dough rest as described. If the mixture is not moist enough to adhere to itself when you first test and squeeze it, you may add beaten egg, 1 teaspoon at a time, or you can use a few drops of water if that is easier and more convenient, until it adheres, and then proceed as directed.

By Electric Mixer

Larger quantities of pasta may be made in an electric mixer. You can successfully make the dough as described by adding the eggs to the flour and using the flat paddle attachment. This will amalgamate the flour and egg, but you will still have to knead it by hand for at least a couple of minutes, dividing the dough into smaller portions if necessary. An exception to this, when you have become comfortable with the process, is to take the dough out in rather large lumps and *immediately* put it into manual or electric pasta rollers, which both knead somewhat as well as roll. It will be elastic and springy but should work just fine.

By Electric Pasta Machine with Dough Hopper

To make the dough in a pasta machine, follow the explicit directions of the manufacturer for both the formula of the dough and the way of making it. Your method must be compatible with the process for which the machine is designed (probably a continuous extrusion) in order to get the best results.

ROLLING THE DOUGH

Only kneading bread by hand comes close to the feeling of triumph you get from rolling pasta dough by hand. It is very personal work, more involving than making a cake or boning a chicken. Rolling pasta dough by hand may seem daunting, but if you see it as a means to making a delicious dish of pasta, you may feel encouraged to try it. You will find you get terrific satisfaction from learning to control the dough. It keeps you motivated and focused as you reach your goal of producing thin, even, springy textured dough that can be cut into a thousand different shapes. After a few tries at rolling dough, you will find you look forward to it.

By Hand

Dough to be rolled by hand should be made a bit softer by deleting 1 or 2 tablespoons of flour from the formula or by adding more egg. The maximum batch anybody can roll out by hand is a 3-egg pasta, due to the natural limits of the length of the roller, the size of the working surface, and the strength of the person. Also, hand rolling calls for a *mattarello* (roller), which is a smooth, long wooden cylinder 2 inches in diameter that you roll with the palms of your hands. This roller has no handles or ball bearings like a regular rolling pin. The dough should be rolled on a clean wood surface, preferably birch or pine, that is not finished in any way (no varnish or oil). The texture of the wood helps to grip the pasta and gives it an invisible patina—a lovely character—in the opinion of some people. (However, I think that's gilding the lily, and I have no personal objection to machine-rolled pasta. In fact, I make it that way all the time. The time saved enables me to do more and more complicated cooking in addition to the pasta dish.)

Dust the surface of the board with flour and place the dough on it. Flatten the ball of dough with your hands, keeping its shape round. Put the rolling pin across the center of the dough and start to roll it away from you. Keep doing that while rotating the dough by quarters or thirds to maintain a circular shape (if it turns out to be oval, don't worry). Remember not to compress the dough or lean on the *mattarello* while you are rolling. Just roll and stretch the dough without flattening it down. Continue with this method until the dough is as thin as you can possibly make it without tearing. It should be less than $1/16$ inch thick. Even though it may seem very thin, remember that it will contract and thicken slightly while drying.

When the dough has reached the approximate desired thickness, you should do one little maneuver that sounds more difficult than it really is. Be sure that the dough is lightly but evenly and sufficiently floured. Place the *mattarello* at the top of the dough sheet. Pull up the top edge of the dough sheet over and around the *mattarello* and roll up about a quarter of the dough sheet (like a paper towel). Put your hands on top of the dough in the center of the *mattarello* and very quickly roll it back and forth about 3 to 4 inches to each side. While continuing to roll, press down firmly with your hands and move them apart, out across the dough, until they reach the opposite ends of the roller.

Take up another quarter of the dough (bringing you to the halfway mark on the sheet) and repeat the process. Then, unfurl the dough sheet, turn it around, and do the same steps from the other end. Repeat the full process twice. The dough is now ready for drying, prior to being cut into shapes.

Put the sheet of pasta on a large cotton or linen sheet or tablecloth, or on your cleaned and floured board. Let it air-dry for about 10 minutes on one side. Then carefully roll it up on the *matterello* to facilitate handling. Unroll it and expose the other side to the air, and let dry for a bit. The total drying time should be about 15 minutes. The dough should feel like a piece of beautiful-quality chamois leather—soft and supple, but strong and not sticky in any way. Time for drying will vary, depending on the humidity of the air and the temperature of the room. This is only a guide. Your experience will lead you to produce better and better pasta every time you make it.

If this initial drying is not done, your noodles will stick together and you will ruin all your hard work. On the other hand, if the dough dries too much, it will crumble and become unusable. A way to test the dryness of the pasta you are going to cut is to fold one edge of the sheet over on itself and squeeze it very hard. If the sheet doesn't stick and separates easily, you may have confidence that the dough will not stick together when the cuts are made. When making pasta on a rainy day, be of good cheer and remember that when all else fails, you can use the hair dryer to help you out.

By Manual or Electric Pasta Rollers
Put the dough through the widest opening of the smooth rollers. Then fold it in thirds like a letter and put it through twice more. Keep reducing the space between the rollers one notch at a time; as you put the pasta through each time, flour it as much as necessary to keep it from sticking. When it is very thin, dry as described. Use your own judgment about the thinness too. Why not take a bit and cook it in boiling water to test your result? If it is too thin and you don't like it that way, bunch it all up and start over. Don't be afraid to experiment; this is the way you will gain precision in your results.

For my personal pasta-making at home, I use small or large Italian manual pasta-rolling machines because of my particular temperament. They do all I've ever wanted them to do, and I think my pasta is considered good. It certainly is eaten with gusto. I have several hand machines, my favorites being Excelsa and Urania in the small size, rolling about a 6-inch width of pasta; and a large Imperia, which goes up to a width of 9 inches. My machines have been in use for almost 40 years, but they look and work as if they were built yesterday. To get the most out of your manual pasta-rolling machines, I suggest you observe the following guidelines:

1. Always secure the machine to a heavy table or countertop for maximum stability before using.
2. Separate the dough into workable portions. Never overload the machine, or it will bind or break the dough—and start to break up its own mechanism.

3. Always start the dough in the widest open position of the rollers, turning the crank at moderate speed. *Do not* try to set world records. Be gentle but firm, and let the machine do its own work.

4. *Never* put stress on the machine. It will do all that you want it to do, but don't abuse it. If necessary, remove the piece of dough and make it a little smaller.

5. Always lower the roller setting one notch at a time to avoid straining the mechanism. The only exceptions to this are if the dough is well-kneaded beforehand, if you are in a hurry, and if your machine is well worked-in and you know its capacities. Then you may reduce the roller spaces by two at a time to speed up the job.

6. Keep your pasta machine scrupulously clean. Use a medium-stiff dry brush to clean the rollers and all the corners and exposed parts. Brush everything thoroughly with the dry brush and use it *only* for this purpose. Then wipe the machine down with a dry cloth. Never, *never* put any water on the machine, not even from a damp cloth, or you will destroy it in short order. Store the machine it its box in a clean location between uses.

7. If properly cleaned with dry brushes and cloths and not stressed beyond its considerable ability, your manual pasta-rolling machine will last a lifetime in perfect condition.

I have seen a home-model electric pasta-rolling machine on the market with rollers about 6 inches wide. Follow the manufacturer's directions scrupulously for the use and care of your machine. The procedure is essentially the same as for the manual model, but with less effort on your part, and the electric machine is even more sensitive and highly tuned than the manual. In pasta stores and restaurants, you can now see much larger electric pasta-rolling machines, which have separate hoppers for mixing and kneading the dough. However, these tend to be a bit too large and expensive for use in the average American home.

By Electric Pasta-Extruder

Home-sized continuous-process-extruding machines are available in the American consumer market. These operate on the principles of modern commercial pasta-making industrial units in Italy today, where a very strong and very firm dough is mixed and then forced into the desired shapes in one continuous process. The manufacturers of the home-sized machines of this type provide explicit directions for the dough formula, which may include hard durum wheat flour or coarse semolina, and possibly some water in addition to the eggs in the egg pasta formula. If the directions for the machine are carefully followed, you will be able to make acceptable pasta of the extrusion type with very little practice. Such machines could be especially desirable for pasta-lovers living in areas where the shapes they want are not available, or where good, dried pastas are hard to find. With a minimum amount of experience or work, you should be able to get reliably good results.

COLORED PASTAS

At the risk of being branded as a heretic, I must tell you that I consider colored pastas, at most, a gimmick. I, for one, am so busy trying to make, to teach, and to eat a truly fine natural egg pasta as a classic *casalinga* (homemade) type that I haven't time to worry about gilding the lily. Only occasionally have I encountered colored pasta in Italy in public eating places. Once in Umbria the pasta was rose-colored, probably from beets, and the color made little difference to my enjoyment of the dish or to my palate's satisfaction. In my opinion it is aesthetically and gastronomically unnecessary to worry about colors in your homemade pasta, with the possible exception of green spinach noodles, which are a nice occasional variation. In a blindfold test, I would not be able to tell the difference in taste between a colored and a plain pasta, except that colored pasta is too often soft and inferior in texture.

If you want to try making some colored pasta, you will find it easier to mix the dough with a food processor than by hand. Take about ½ cup of cooked spinach, tomato, or whatever vegetable color you want and squeeze it as dry as you can in paper towels. (This is easier if you have steamed the vegetable in as little water as possible.) You can also dry it by tossing it in a dry frying pan, or with the hair dryer; better yet, cook it the day before and let it air-dry overnight. Purée the vegetable in the food processor; add the flour and mix well before adding the egg, as a guide to the amount of egg the mixture will take. You may have to reduce the amount of egg lest the dough becomes too soft.

Dried vegetable powders pulverized to the fineness of face powder are used in making commercial colored pastas. If they ever become available on the consumer market, it will be possible to make colored pasta at home with more reliable results. Once the dough is made, colored pasta-making proceeds exactly as the plain.

Incidentally, my remarks about colored pasta do not apply to the natural whole wheat pasta used a lot in and around Venice. To make this, try replacing up to 70 percent of the unbleached white flour in your formula with whole-wheat flour, and proceed as usual. You will have to develop the right amounts on an ad hoc basis, incorporating as much whole wheat as the pasta will take.

Pasta Cuts

Since its basic primitive beginnings, Italian pasta has acquired an almost bewildering variety of shapes and forms which are used in countless different ways. No other food in history comes to mind that has ever been applied in a fraction of so many different versions. How and why this came to pass is difficult to know for sure.

Perhaps it is due in part to the fundamental diversity of the Italian people, who were only unified by Garibaldi into one nation in the 1860s. The differences among the Italians even today are seen by sociologists as far greater in extent and more fundamental in kind than among the inhabitants of any other country of comparable size. All Italians have in common, however, a profound respect for good, basic food ingredients, perhaps because in their overpopulated homeland these have always been in short supply.

Another reason for the many riotous shapes of pasta may be that the Italians are always ready to rejoice in *abbondanza* (plenty) when it comes to food, because it represents to them the joy of living and the goodness of life. Even medical studies of the remarkable health of Italian pasta-eaters comment on their deep enjoyment of the food they eat as a significant element of their general well-being.

To get to know the hundreds of cuts and shapes of Italian pasta is no small undertaking. The challenge is compounded by the fact that the same shapes may be called by different names in different parts of Italy. If you're eating tagliatelle in Bologna, your counterpart in Rome would be eating fettuccine—exactly the same ribbon cut. There are legends galore about how the pasta shapes developed; of course, everyone knows that the stuffed tortellini was originally modeled after Venus's navel.

Chifferi

Suffice it to say that all people of all ages like, at times, to play. A little knowledge can be a dangerous thing, but at the risk of oversimplifying an approach to describing Italy's hundreds of pasta cuts, let's start out with the simplest and best-known shapes we can make ourselves or obtain readily in America.

Strozzapreti

Flat Ribbon Pastas

The narrowest strips are those measuring up to 1 ½ inches wide are called flat ribbon pastas:

Lingue di passero (sparrow's tongues)
Bavettini (collar or tie)
Linguine (tongues)
Bavette (larger collar; at least ⅛ inch wide)
Tagliarini (little cuts) or *fettuccine* (ribbons)
Pizzoccheri (rustic buck-wheat noodles; 4-inch lengths, ¼ inch wide)
Trenette (trains) or *lasagnette* or *fettuccine* (a larger, alternative ribbon)
Pappardelle (no one knows what this name means; about 1 inch wide)
Lasagne (possibly means clumsy, from "dolt"; up to 1¼ inch to 1½ inches wide). Note that in the past lasagne were sometimes square or oblong pieces of pasta dough, often with rippled edges, which were layered at random with a cooked filling in an *unbaked* dish.

Orecchiette

You will probably find two or three of these widths among the dies supplied with your manual or electric pasta-rolling machine. To make these ribbon pastas, simply take your pasta sheets, prepared and dried as directed, and run them through the rollers with the desired die attachment. To make the very narrow and very wide widths for which no dies are available, roll up your pasta sheet loosely in the shape of a roll of paper towels, and cut across it with a knife by hand to the width desired. You can, of course, hand cut all of the widths if you don't have the rollers and dies.

Spugnole

One caution: Never make your fresh ribbon pastas more than 12 inches long, as they will bind up during cutting. Don't worry about

Taccozzette

waste in trimming up your pasta sheets, as there is a use for the scraps known as *malfatti* (poorly made), which can be dried and set aside to be used in broths and soups. Also, if you wish, you can use a fluted wheel dough-cutter to crimp the edges of your larger ribbons and lasagne for a more finished look.

Once cut, your ribbon pastas may be cooked at once and eaten fresh; dried (hung on the back of a chair, a towel rack, or any similar arrangement); floured as necessary and cooked later; or dried,

Bucati

floured (some prefer to use rice flour, as it's drier than wheat flour), and stored. Fresh egg pasta may be kept in the refrigerator for 2 days. If completely dried and placed in a bag or a box, it can be stored for about as long as commercial pasta.

Pasta Tubes and Rods, Long and Short
In the old days, thin tube pastas were made by wrapping a long, narrow strip of pasta lengthwise around a knitting needle, pressing the flap to seal it closed, and then withdrawing the needle. My cousin Mary, who lives near Rome, makes a similar pasta but she uses a stalk of wheat devoid of wheat berries. On one of my

Rigatoni

trips to Italy I found a charming old lady making *garganelli* (gulps or bites), sometimes called *pasta alla pettine* (pasta made on a comb), by hand in a small pasta shop in Imola, near

Bologna. This is a short pasta rolled diagonally around a small, round-ended wooden stick against a *pettine* (a cane comb), which gives it a slightly *rigati* (grooved) texture. It is actually a small *mostaccioli* (mustache), a name better known in America. The old lady made me a gift of one of her own stick-and-comb sets, but I, like most others, lack the time for such detailed hand production. She, of course, made the *garganelli* from small strips of dough with dazzling speed.

Rods and tubes are made in commercial dried pastas in Italy today by the industrial continuous-extrusion process. Some of the same shapes can be found in commercial dried American pastas. Some of them can be made fresh at home with the electric pasta-extrusion machines (check their available dies).

For the best texture, dry freshly made rods and tubes on a clean cloth for about 1 hour

Pizzoccheri

before cooking them. If you dry them completely, you can store them in a paper bag for a month or two. Rods and tubes include the following long shapes, listed from smallest to largest:

Capellini (hairs; cylindrical pasta, very tiny)
Vermicelli (worms; a little larger than capellini)
Spaghettini (small strings; cylindrical)
Spaghetti (normal strings; a little larger than spaghettini)
Bucati (pierced twisted strings)
Bucatini (pierced) or *fischietti* (whistles; smallest of the tubes)

Strozzapreti (priest stranglers; irregular tubes about 4½ inches long)

Perciateli (tubes)

Macaroni (tubes; a bit larger)

Ditalini (little fingers; short tube about ¼ inch long)

Ziti (large tubes)

Ziti rigati (large tubes; grooved)

Then there are the short cylinders and tubes with plain or grooved texture:

Chifferi (half-moon or curved tubes with ridges)

Bombolotti (short, smooth cylinders)

Penne (quills; diagonal tubes)

Mostaccioli (mustaches; diagonal tubes)

Rigatoni (grooved tubes)

There are also the curved short "elbows," which may be made from any of these shapes.

Fancy-Shaped Pastas

With the exception of the *farfalle* (butterflies) and *fiochetti* (small bows or bow ties), which are pinched from flat pieces and can be made by hand if you have the time, these fancy concave shapes are best made today by machines that force the extruded dough through special dies:

Lumache (snail shells)

Cappelli de preti (small priests' hats)

Conchiglie (seashells; several sizes from small to jumbo)

Orecchiette (little ears)

Creste di gallo (cocks' combs)

Taccozzette (heel-shaped, diamond-like flat pieces)

Spugnole (sponges; ruffled half circles)

Fusilli (twists)

Rotelle (wheels)

To make the butterflies and bows by hand, cut rectangular pieces approximately 2 inches by 1 inch, from your pasta sheet, using a fluted wheel if you want a fancy edge, and simply pinch them together in the middle. You can also round the corners of the rectangles if you wish. Dry 30 to 40 minutes before cooking.

Small Pastas for Broths and Soups

It would not make sense to attempt the tiniest pasta shapes by hand, especially because a large number of them tend to be commercially available. They can add a great deal to broths and soups. If you cook pasta in broth, you should plan to eat it right away. If you leave the soup for even 30 minutes, the pasta will swell up, absorb the broth, and become flaccid and overcooked. If you plan to use the broth another day, cook the pasta separately, drain it well, toss with oil to coat lightly, and store covered in the refrigerator. When the broth is hot, add the amount of pasta you want, wait until the pasta is heated through, then enjoy it.

Here is a list of some of the popular and best-known tiny pastas:

Acini de pepe (peppercorns)

Alfabeto (letters of the alphabet)

Anelli (rings)

Anellini (little rings)

Anellini rigati (grooved rings)

Capelli d'angelo (angels' hairs)

Cappelli di pagliaccio (clowns' hats)
Chicchi di riso (grains of rice)
Conchigliette or *maruzzine* (tiny shells)
Coralli (coral)
Funghini (little mushrooms)
Orzo (barley)
Pastina (tiny dough)
Perline microscopici (tiny pearls)
Pulcini (little chicks)
Semi de mele (apple seeds)
Semi de melone (melon seeds)
Stelline (little stars)
Tubettini (tiny tubes)

   Clearly, pastas are named for their shapes, and this category opens a world of imaginative educational opportunities for children. One soup pasta that you can make by hand is *pasta gratugiata* (grated pasta), because of its less defined shape. Prepare fresh egg pasta dough; let it rest 10 minutes, loosely covered in clear plastic warp; then grate it on a flat, large-holed grater. Let the gratings rest uncovered for 40 minutes; then cook them for about 6 minutes and add to your soups. This is another excellent way to use up pasta trimmings.

Stuffed Pastas

Some of the *paste ripiene* (stuffed pastas) that make a major contribution to the Italian pasta repertory:

Cappelletti (little hats worn by bishops and
  cardinals)
Agnolotti ("little lambs"; round ravioli)
Cannelloni (large reeds)

Manicotti (small muffs)
Ravioli (small, square pillows)
Tortellini (small filled rings)

   With fillings of cheese, spinach, meat, or chicken, and with sauces, these pastas make excellent and appropriate main-dish meals. They can and should be made from sheets of fresh egg pasta dough *before* it has been dried, and the results are definitely worth the extra effort. All of them start with circles or squares of pasta that are rolled or pressed around fillings and fashioned into their special shapes (see Stuffed Pastas, page 92).

   These freshly made stuffed pasta can now be bought in pasta stores and Italian delicatessens in many American communities. Some of them are also available in the supermarkets as frozen prepared dishes. There are a couple of other options available to you to assemble at home. *Manicotti* shells can be bought in dried form, sometimes specially treated so that they need not be boiled before stuffing and baking. I've tried these and they are not bad, especially for entertaining in larger numbers when you are short of time to make your own by hand. Also the *conchiglie* (jumbo shells) and the *ziti* (large tubes), if available in dried form, can be boiled and then filled with delicious fresh homemade stuffing, sauced, and baked with highly successful results (see recipes on pages 100 and 102).

Gnocchi

Gnocchi, or dumplings, were possibly the first primitive pasta shapes ever made. However, today gnocchi are made of so many things other than pasta dough (potatoes, ricotta cheese, polenta, semolina, and so on) that I am not including them in this pasta collection.

Some Tips for Using and Serving Pasta

● Fresh pasta, which (especially when rolled) is distinctly firm and springy yet deliciously tender, will absorb sauces more readily than commercial dried pasta.
● The delicacy of fresh pasta deserves the lightest, least assertive saucing.
● Tubular and concave pasta shapes are actually designed to trap sauces. Use them when you want to eat a lot of sauce in each bite.
● Delicate sauces are best served with delicate pasta.
● A rich sauce should be served with a flat pasta, or a shape that will not trap or accumulate too much of the sauce in each bite.
● The taste of pasta varies with the thickness and texture of the particular cut.
● While one school of thought holds that you should drink water with pasta and no wine until afterwards, the majority of Italians enjoy wine with their pasta.
● The wines to accompany pasta are chosen to go well with the particular sauce used. In Italy, a wine of the same region as the pasta dish is generally served, but I like to be adventurous and pair wines and pastas from different regions.

Italians have brought the making and eating of pasta to a fine art. The more deeply you become involved in the experience yourself, the better you will be able to orchestrate the broad range of opportunities pasta offers to satisfy your own taste and enjoyment of eating.

Cooking Pasta

Boil, Boil, Toil and Trouble! The first two words apply. The others are inaccurate where pasta is concerned. Here are some of the golden rules that will get you through the cooking of pasta without toil or trouble.

1. Use lots of water, so that the pasta can float freely while cooking. You should allow at least 4 to 5 quarts of water per pound of pasta. Too little water prevents the pasta from cooking evenly, and the pieces may stick together as a result.
2. Bring the water to a galloping boil.
3. When the water is boiling briskly, add the salt, preferably noniodized. (If the salt is added before the water boils, it may leave a residual taste of phenol on delicate pastas.) Add 1 teaspoon of salt for every quart of water.
4. Drop the pasta into the boiling water. Long pastas should be in manageable lengths. The commercial dried pastas, especially, will grow larger during cooking. To get very long pastas into the pot, grasp a bundle of them at one end; submerge the other end of the bundle in the boiling water; as the submerged end of the pasta bundle softens, gradually release your hold and the rest of the bundle of long pastas will slide into the pot of boiling water without breaking.

5. Watch the pasta carefully. Fresh homemade egg pasta will cook in seconds or minutes. Commercial dried pastas generally cook in 7 to 8 minutes depending on size. You can be guided to some extent by the directions on the package, but it is still essential to watch the pasta very closely as it cooks and to test it frequently for doneness.

6. Pasta is done when it tests al dente (to the tooth), is tender but firm, still bitable and not mushy, and has no taste of flour.

7. Remove the pasta from the boiling water immediately. It can be lifted out of the water with a pasta rake or a slotted spoon, or it can be drained in a colander. Be sure the pasta remains nicely wet, or it will absorb too much sauce and probably will stick together.

8. Pasta to be served with a sauce should be eaten immediately. The sauce should be ready and waiting. The bowls or plates should be heated. Toss the pasta in some of the sauce (use a separate heated serving bowl, or the empty pot in which it was cooked), serve it and pass additional sauce and cheese, as the recipe directs.

9. Boiled pasta to be baked should be under-cooked in the boiling, as it will cook more when baked in the sauce. Also, the pasta can be cooled and the boiling arrested by plunging it into cold water. This is the one and only type of cooking in which you would do this to the pasta.

10. Stuffed pastas, such as tortellini, ravioli, and pansoti, are cooked the same way as the ones above—in other words, in boiling salted water. Since they are made with fresh pasta, they will cook faster than dry packaged pasta, usually 5 minutes should do it. Test one at 4 minutes and you will be able to judge the timing better. If the stuffed pastas are frozen, proceed as directed but add 1 minute to the cooking time. I like to scoop stuffed pastas out of the cooking water with a big spoon with large holes. This keeps them from falling apart.

Undercook the dough before you stuff pastas that are to be baked, such as cannelloni or pasta shells. Otherwise they will overcook and become soggy. Do not pack them too tightly in the baking dish; leave about 1/4 inch between them to allow for expansion.

The Pasta-Maker's Pantry
(La Dispensa del Pastaio)

ONLY RECENTLY I learned something I never knew before, although I have been cooking all my life. The word *recipe* is not an English or French word, as I had always believed, but actually the Latin word for "procure" in its imperative form. This suggests the functions of marketing and the *mis en place* in French or *a posto* in Italian, or the assembly of ingredients so critical to the working cook.

I want to suggest a few basic items for you to stock up on. You may want to keep the nonperishables on hand regularly. You would probably be wise to identify sources for the perishables where you will be able to find them when you need them instead of finding yourself stuck at the last minute. If there are no stores where you live that carry the special Italian items, consult the list of mail-order sources on page 128.

Many of the imported specialties are a bit expensive. However, most of them are well worth whatever you can afford to pay, as remarkably small quantities will go a long way toward giving the true taste of Italy to your pasta dishes. Of course, I think you should have imported Parmigiano-Reggiano cheese, imported pecorino cheese, and of course, extra virgin olive oil. But, if you can't get these ingredients, I would rather you make the dishes with the materials you have at hand and appreciate the concept of the recipe than not make it at all,

even though you might miss the high points in flavor that are to be derived from using the authentic ingredients. (Not everyone can go to see the Mona Lisa, but a reasonable facsimile can still activate some of the emotional machinery needed to have a satisfying experience.)

EVERYDAY ITEMS

- Flour, all-purpose, unbleached
- Whole milk
- Eggs, U.S. grade A
- Butter, always unsalted
- Sea salt
- Whole black pepper for grinding
- Heavy cream
- Garlic
- Onions
- Scallions
- Bread crumbs, dried and unseasoned
- Tomatoes
- Spinach. Fresh is best; frozen will do in some cases.
- Red and green bell peppers, in season.

CANNED GOODS

- Tomatoes, canned and unsalted. The 28-ounce (1-pound 12-ounce) size (approximately $3\frac{1}{2}$ cups) is most useful. Test to make sure you find a reliable brand with a thick puréed pack, not a watery pack.

- Tomato paste. Tubes are handy and keep well in the refrigerator after opening.
- Tomato purée.
- Tuna, packed in oil. The imported Italian variety, if you can find it, is definitely worth the cost.
- Anchovy fillets, packed in salt if available, or packed in olive oil.
- Capers, the large Sicilian type, if possible, bulk-packed in salt, if you can find them.
- Chopped clams. Make sure they are not sandy.
- Extra virgin olive oil (imported Italian is best).

HERBS, SPICES, AND NUTS

In general, fresh herbs are more pungent than dried; whole spices freshly ground are much more flavorful than those preground; and nuts should be as fresh as possible and stored in the freezer.

- Basil
- Bay leaves
- Fennel seeds
- Oregano
- Sage
- Nutmeg
- Red pepper flakes
- Ground white pepper
- Pine nuts
- Walnut meats
- Fresh Italian (or flat-leaf) parsley

SPECIALTY ITEMS

- Pancetta, Italian-style salt-cured (unsmoked) bacon. If you can't find it, regular bacon may be used after first poaching it in water for a few minutes to reduce the smoky flavor, or lean salt pork soaked in cold water for 1 hour to remove some of the salt.
- Prosciutto, salt-cured, unsmoked Italian ham. Have it thinly sliced at the store. Imported Italian Prosciutto di Parma is the best and is usually available at specialty delicatessens.
- Mortadella, an Italian-style sausage, a kind of bologna, thinly sliced.
- Olives, Sicilian black or green, or Gaeta, or calamata. Unfortunately, commercially packed American olives do not approach these olives' taste and will not give you the result you want in the recipes calling for olives.
- Dried porcini mushrooms, imported from Italy and well worth the price. In case you enjoy wild mushroom hunting, these are the *Boletus edulis* species, which can be found in a lot of areas in the United States.

WINES

Pasta dishes, being fairly light for the most part, call for uncomplicated dry, young white and red wines. Of course, there are exceptions to this as there are to all rules, and some pastas certainly can stand up to heavier and more full-bodied wines. Most of the large production of Italian wine fits the major criterion for use with pasta dishes, in that this wine is generally made to be drunk while young, with little or no aging. More and more of the regional wines of Italy are now being imported. They tend to be well priced and quite suitable for use with pasta in the United States, just as they are used in Italy.

With the pasta recipes I recommend wines by their generic names or types. You should find that sufficient to help you find the ones I suggest as the most suitable. Your own taste will surely differ from mine. Buy accordingly.

Any remarks I make about wines, whether they be Italian, French, or Californian, should be taken with a fifth of the stuff, as it will make it all easier and better. Of wines I know not a great deal. Mostly the knowledge extends to remembering the types I have liked in the past and to trying to get more as I want it. I also "know" by some genetic programming what is acceptable in Italian wines, and this enables me to enjoy almost all of them for their own characteristics and merits.

Not being a wine scholar and, I might add, not having a good memory, I find it especially difficult to discuss wines except in the most general terms, probably best expressed as a wine-drinking philosophy. My colleagues who have vast experience and knowledge of wine-making and wine-drinking are blessed, according to them, with good memories. Therefore, when they speak of wines, they can often say, quite accurately, "This wine is not as good as the 'sixty-eight, which was also grown on the southeast slope of the highest hill in the vineyard." Of course all these factors do make a difference in the wine at drinking time.

Then there is the method of making the stuff. Steel tanks, controlled fermentation, killing off wild yeast and introducing a new one which,

like DNA, will give you certain predictable characteristics. Can you imagine what progress is doing to the wine industry? You'll soon be able to order up a 2001 vintage with blue eyes and blond hair. This is the science of wine-making and drinking. I will talk mostly about the soul of wine-drinking.

The Italians are fast adapting the wine-growing and wine-making that the French and Californians have used for such a long time. They want to compete on more objective grounds with the French and California wines. Italy currently supplies so much wine to the French and Americans that it seems impossible that the country could produce so much. The wine scientists are generally critical of Italian wines because they compare them to the French and California wines. This is already an error. You can't taste an orange and then complain that it just doesn't measure up to that apple you ate the other day. Italian wines are as complex as any others, but different. As long as you remember that they are different from other wines, you will be able to enjoy them to the fullest.

Many wineries in the southern part of Italy were strictly producers of "cutting" wines or wines that could be added to other wines to give body, or different characteristics. Over time, many of these wineries realized that their product was so good and in such demand, they began making wines in their own style and using their names on the label. Decades later, they have made a great business of supplying excellent wine to the world.

In Italy, wine *is* food. It is as simple as that.

Italian wines tend to be a little lower in alcohol content than the wines of other countries. They are often sharper (I'd say "gutsy") and they like to be lured out into the open. As a general rule, let red wines "breathe" for at least an hour before serving. There is an Italian saying that if you want to treat your guests well, open the wine the night before you expect them.

Wine-drinking is a national pastime for sure in Italy, but there is a very low incidence of alcoholism—one of the lowest in the world. There is also very long life expectancy in Italy. I'm convinced that this is because of the pasta and wine consumption. Wine in Italy is appreciated very much on its own, but it is almost always served together with something to eat. An afternoon glassful will often be accompanied by hard, tasty cookies and a basket of fruit. When making a shopping list or making up a menu, wine is there along with the peppers, pasta, veal, cheese, and bread, all equal partners in the care and happiness of the stomach and soul. You don't need to be a mathematician to calculate that in the formula of, say, $20 for a nice, home-cooked meal for four people and $10 or $12 or even more for a bottle of good wine in America there is a horrible imbalance. Wine-drinking here is more of a hobby or a sport than in Italy, and, as a result, we have fewer wines available that are priced in line with other food costs. Italians would not tolerate this. Many still make their own wine at home. While I don't like wine snobs, I find nothing wrong with an Italian who generously offers a glass of his home specialty and proudly says, "I make the best!"

White wines are also enjoyed in Italy, but they are outnumbered by the reds two to one. There are more and more whites now being produced of excellent quality and low price. A bottle of chilled white wine with some prosciutto and melon or figs is sheer heaven! Fish and chicken, both eaten extensively in Italy, are easy partners to white wine. But look out: good, deep, chest-thumping red wines are equally at home with fish or chicken in a restaurant. Some time when you are eating fish or chicken in a restaurant, look the waiter in the eye and say, with authority, "I want red wine," and then enjoy your meal.

For those of you who are wise scholars of good wine and have good taste and good memories, think of me often and toast me with a great wine, which I will probably never have (unless you give it to me). I will toast you, too, because of the time and attention you give to a very important food. We can co-exist very well. As an example of the importance of wine in the life of Italians, I can cite the following. Italy is the largest wine producer in the world. It is also the largest wine consumer in the world. Italy produces more types and varieties of wine than any other nation—1,500 in fact. The best known of these number more than 420. Italy, a tiny country with a fraction of the population of the United States, produces about four times as much wine as America, and supplies more wine to America than any other foreign country. One last fact tells the story better than I can. Italy produces about 1,585,200,000 gallons of wine per year (that's 7,926,000,000 bottles!). Fifty-six percent of this production is exported. Forty-four percent, or 3,534,000,000 bottles, is drunk by the Italians themselves, and by the tourists who flock to Italy to enjoy its many charms, at the rate of approximately 62 bottles per capita annually.

A few years ago, Sicily was in the midst of a wine-making revolution (not a political one for a change). Sicily, being the poorest region of Italy economically, was also the last to be able to modernize its wine-making so that more reliable wines could emerge year after year. Now it is a different story. Sicilian wines are excellent and many of them have worldwide reputations. In a major white wine tasting in France a few years ago, the Sicilian-made Chardonnay from Regaleali took first prize over the best of the French! That shot was heard all over the world. Many southern Italian wines are now on a par with the best northern Italian wines, which means they compare with the best French and California wines. In general, Italian wines still offer the best dollar-to-value ratio available.

GLOSSARY OF ITALIAN WINES

The following is a very short list of Italian wines I believe you will enjoy. They are merely drops in the vast ocean of Italian wines, but they are all excellent and worthy of your appraisal.

Aglianico—This is said to be the oldest of known grapes still botanically unchanged over the last 2,000 years. Some of the finest examples of Aglianico wines are made by Mastroberardino in Campania and Fratelli d'Angelo in Basilicata. The wine is red, rich, earthy, and mouth-filling, a treat whether drunk by itself or with game and mushroom dishes or nuts.

Alcamo Bianco—From the area around Alcamo in western Sicily comes a light, pale yellow wine that is made primarily with Catarratto grapes. It is versatile, enjoyable as a sipping wine but very good with pasta dishes with fish, and soothing dishes such as fettuccine with butter. Serve it nicely chilled and it will do good service at your table.

Arneis—In Piedmont, which is near Alba, this wine is called Arneis, meaning hard. It is said that this wine is so difficult to make that it needs a human in attendance throughout its fermentation, which sometimes takes 3 months. The old farmers used to make it and it was variable indeed until Bruno Giacosa finally made it stable and very drinkable. It is florid, fresh, and delightful served slightly chilled.

Barbaresco—One of the great wines of Italy from the Piedmont area around the town this wine is named after. The grape is Nebbiolo. The wine is noble and goes with almost any food you can name; I love it with baked pasta casseroles and hearty dishes such as Fusilli delle Madonie.

Barolo—A big dry red wine, made from the Nebbiolo grape, that needs aging. In my opinion, it is best after 10 years, although the recent vintages are drinkable much sooner—say after 3 or so years of aging. A great wine in every way. One of the best of the Piedmont region, and all of Italy. Some call it the king of Italian wines.

Barbera—Made from the same Nebbiolo grape, but made near the town of Barbera. Less alcoholic than Barolo, but has very good, strong character. Dry and full-bodied with red garnet color.

Brunello di Montalcino—Made from Brunello grapes (a relative of Sangiovese grapes), this is a rather recent wine on the Italian scene, being only around 100 years old. It is quite expensive and must be barrel-aged at least 4 years before being bottled. It could easily age 50 years thereafter, but don't wait. Use it as you would a Chianti Riserva.

Cabernet Sauvignon—In Piedmont this grape has been revived. The wine is very smooth, velvety, dry, and tasty, as is the one from the Trentino-Alto Adige region. These are first-class wines, and I love them with roasted meat, tomato, and cream dishes, or I sip them while eating bread and walnuts.

Cannonau di Sardegna—Made all over the island of Sardinia with Cannonau grapes, this wine can support very high alcohol levels without losing any of the profound flavors of earth, leather, and nuts. This powerful wine is not for the faint-hearted but it is exceptional with baked pasta, game, and mushroom dishes, and terrific with heavily flavored cheeses such as Gorgonzola or pecorino.

Chardonnay—This overwhelmingly popular white wine is made in several places in Italy, from Friuli to Sicily. It resembles nothing found in California, where the wine has the intense flavors of new oak barrels. The Italian-style Chardonnays have been described as lean and mean; I don't agree. They taste fresh, elegant, and are perfect with prosciutto, cream, and shellfish pasta dishes. Be sure to try this wine, which is also good for just sipping.

Chianti—Surely the most famous Tuscan wine in America. It is a marvelous wine that can be used with almost any food, or drunk just on its own. Some young Chianti wines are made to be drunk very young, and, of course, then there is the Riserva which is at least 3 years old and made from Sangiovese, Canaiolo Black, and a few Malvasia grapes. It is better to let this ruby red gem age for 4 or more years before quaffing.

Cirò Rosato—A very old wine from Calabria. The major grape used is Galioppo. This is a velvety dry, versatile wine, and I love to drink it with pecorino cheese and bread. It is an excellent wine with baked pasta dishes.

Corvo Rosso—It is made by Duca di Salaparuta in Sicily and is really a brand name for several kinds of wine they make. For the Rosso the main grapes are Inzolia, Trebbiano, and Catarratto. This is one of the most reliable wines there is. Medium in weight, dry and tasty. It is good with meat or tomato-based dishes. I like it sometimes with cream-based dishes as well.

Frascati—The Castelli Romani (Roman Castles) area around Rome, which produces many light delicious white and red wines, gives us Frascati made from Malvasia, Tuscan Trebbiano, and Greco (yellow Trebbiano).

Traditionally, it was drunk very young, straight out of the barrel (some is still delivered that way in Rome from a horse-drawn wagon). What we get here is a modern version made to stand the rigors of travel across the sea. The old type is from Renaissance times. The modern Frascati is delicate, so don't use it with highly flavored dishes.

Gattinara—Piedmont, the home of so many fabulous wines, is also the home of this excellent wine made from Nebbiolo grapes. It is an old wine that has suffered a bit in the past from careless production, but now it is reaching its potential as a truly great red wine. It hints of violets and sometimes of tar. This is a sure winner with gutsy pasta dishes that feature olives, tomatoes, and anchovies.

Lacryma Christi del Vesuvio—This elegant wine from Campania, near Mount Vesuvius, is one of the best dry whites Italy offers. It is a good sipping wine and is excellent with robust dishes, such as Spaghetti alla Puttanesca.

Lambrusco—From the breadbasket of Italy, the Po Valley, this wine can be awful, especially if it is sweet, the type you will most likely encounter. Try to get a dry Lambrusco and drink it with a very rich food such as Tagliatelle alla Bolognese and you will see what a good balance it can give to the meal. Whether sweet or dry it is slightly spritzy, but it subsides as you drink it.

Merlot—Made in many parts of northern and central Italy, Merlot is a medium-light wine with hints of various herbs and is good with dishes such as fowl, baked pasta dishes, or fish and tomato dishes when you don't want a white wine.

Montepulciano d'Abruzzo—This is one of my favorite Abruzzese wines for all-around use made from grapes of the same name. If you have limited budget, but want many of the attributes of a big-name, high-priced wine, try this one with meat-based dishes, minestrone, and cheese dishes.

Orvieto—Umbria gives us this white wine, which is dry, intense, and clear. It is made from the Trebbiano grape and some Tuscan Malvasia, Verdello, and Grechetto. There is red, but you are not likely to encounter it. The dry white is good with a variety of dishes.

Pinot Bianco—This wine comes from many areas in Italy, but most of it comes from the north and some good ones come from the central part. It is well liked by most people who drink white wines, and it is very good with dishes such as Spaghetti alla Carbonara or Pappardelle con i Porcini.

Pinot Grigio—Gray pinot grapes make this dry, tart, delicious white wine from the Friuli–Venezia Giulia region. Drink it before dinner and pair it with pork roast and some good stout cheeses.

Regaleali Rosso—From Sclafani Bagni in Sicily is a high-quality, value-priced, reliable wine. It's named for the winery that produces it and is made from Nerello Mascalese and

Perricone grapes. It is dry, earthy, and easy to drink, especially with duck or smoky-flavored dishes.

Rosato del Salento—From the Salento Peninsula in Puglia, this rose wine is dry and delightful. Made primarily from Negroamaro grapes, it is a good all-around wine but especially good with clam dishes and roasted vegetables.

Soave—The famous white wine from Verona, known since the thirteenth century. Made from Garganega and Trebbiano di Soave grapes, it is dry and crisp and can be used very well with a large variety of foods.

Valpolicella—A wine from the Veneto region around Verona. Made mainly from Corvina, Rondinella, and Molinara grapes, it is red, warm, smooth, and dry with a *touch* of sweetness.

Verdicchio—From the Marches region we have a lovely crisp white wine made mostly from Verdicchio grapes. It has been noted for its quality since Roman times. It is delicious with fish or roasted game birds. I like it with polenta.

Vermentino—This Sardinian white is grown in several parts of the island, and the one from Gallura is especially appealing. It is light, very subtly fruity, and perfect with prosciutto and cream dishes, as well as with shellfish.

Vino Nobile di Montepulciano—This red wine, which was known in the fourteenth century, is made like the Chinati Riserva, but it must be aged at least 4 years. Delicious with roasts, good stout cheeses, and pears and apples. Don't confuse this wine with Montepulciano d'Abruzzo.

CHEESES

The cheeses of Italy are as varied and complex as the wines and far more difficult to discuss. One can start by saying that the Italians have not traditionally been large milk drinkers, which may stem from an earlier lack of facilities for pasteurization. However, they make up for it by eating a great deal of many different types of cheese. Furthermore, they milk not only cows, but also sheep, goats, and even water buffaloes in order to produce a wide variety of cheeses.

Availability of these cheeses in America is also a problem linked to regulations around pasteurization and aging required for import. It is slowly being worked out, and more good Italian cheeses are gradually showing up in this country. The Italians also have a lot to learn about shipping *con moto*, packing to protect their products from damage in transit, and other logistics to permit their cheeses to become a viable export product. They are more used to taking each day as it comes, and they have only recently begun to think in terms of sending their most precious, delicate, and perishable products so far from home. I now believe that they are modifying some of their cheeses to enable them to travel better and longer, while still maintaining their outstanding goodness. However, the taste of Italian cheese on its home soil is still a richer and more exciting experience than sampling the export product. When you travel in Italy, I hope you will go directly to the store and buy and taste the cheese so that you will experience it at its finest.

GLOSSARY OF ITALIAN CHEESES

Even a brief general discussion of Italian cheeses would fill a big book. The following list of cheeses will give you a nice selection of those that travel best to America and a brief description of their characteristics. You are more likely to find these available than some of the other delicious but more obscure Italian cheeses.

Caciocavallo—Made from cow's milk, this "horse cheese" is named such because two balls of cheese resembling gourds are tied together with a piece of raffia to look like saddlebags draped over the haunches of a horse. It is cured for several weeks or longer and is firm and very tasty with strong earthy flavors. It is suitable for cooking or grating over pasta or simply eating out of hand.

Fontina Val d' Aosta—This cow's milk cheese is sometimes called Valdostana. It is Alpine cheese used for melting or making fondue, and is very pungent, with a rich nutty flavor. Do not confuse it with Danish fontina, which is good but not in Italian dishes.

Gorgonzola—Made from cow's milk. One of the most prized of all Italian cheeses, this famous "blue" cheese is actually green. It is a natural mold that comes from its curing in dank caves. Sharp, fragrant, and creamy-crumbly, it is utterly delicious with apples, pears, and peaches. Wonderful to cook with, too.

Mascarpone—Made from cow's milk. This 88 percent–butterfat cheese is like cheese-flavored butter. It is slightly tart, and an absolute treat, if you can get it, as it's extremely perishable and difficult to transport from Italy. Domestic mascarpone does not hold a candle to the imported Italian ones.

Mozzarella—Made from water buffalo milk. The imported one is very pungent, expensive, and difficult to find. It is rather stringy. Domestic mozzarella can be fine, but it is made from cow's milk and does not have the lively flavor of the Italian cheese. Used a lot in cooking, it is indispensable in Italian dishes.

Parmesan—Made from cow's milk. This cheese is made domestically and thus is reasonably priced. It is good for pasta fillings and baked dishes. Do not store it grated; use it freshly grated whenever you need it.

Parmigiano-Reggiano—Made from cow's milk. Indeed, this is the king of cheese used all over Italy. The best comes from around Parma, hence its name. True, it is more expensive than other Parmesan-type cheese but is worth the money. It is smooth, luscious, superbly flavored, and delicious to eat out of hand as well as grated on pasta. It will keep well in the refrigerator for several months. Grate it only when you are ready to use it.

Pecorino—Made from sheep's milk. Another indispensable cheese for pasta and meat stuffings. Also known by its place of origin, such as Romano or Sardo (Sardinian), because pecorino is the generic name. It has a salty and forceful flavor. A great cheese.

Provolone—Made from water buffalo milk, and sometimes cow's milk. Has great fragrance and crumbly texture. A good ally in the kitchen because it brings out the flavor of other ingredients.

Ricotta—Made from sheep's milk, and sometimes goat's milk. In the United States it is made of cow's milk. This is another indispensable cheese in Italian cooking. It is equally at home in a pasta dish like lasagne or ravioli, or in a dessertlike cannoli or ricotta pudding. Ricotta looks a little like cottage cheese, but it's lighter, fluffier, and sweeter. Lovely tasting and so versatile.

Ricotta Salata—Like ricotta, this cheese is also made from sheep's milk. First, the ricotta is slightly dried in a basket. Then, when it is quite firm, it's soaked in salt brine. It has a piquant taste, and is good to eat with bread as well as shredded on pasta dishes.

Taleggio (Stracchino)—Made from cow's milk. Specific cheese from its namesake city near Bergamo. One of many *Stracca* or "tired" cheeses. Supposedly, the cows moved from pasture to pasture and became tired. When milked, they gave good but different-tasting milk. It was probably the different grasses they ate rather than their state of fatigue that made the change. This cheese is soft, creamy, and almost nutty in flavor. It is an excellent eating cheese and a good companion to almost anything you want.

[Recipes]

Basic Sauces
(Salsa di Base)

Salsa di Pomodoro Stracotto

(Slow Tomato Sauce)

MAKES 2 1/2 QUARTS

This is the classic approach to the richer, heavier, and traditionally darker-colored tomato sauce, which is cooked slowly for a long time. In Italy, fresh sun-ripened tomatoes, usually the smaller pear-shaped type, are preserved for use between seasons by sun-drying, which is preferred to canning. The fresh tomatoes are split, lightly salted, strung into ropes, and hung outdoors until dried naturally by sun and air. Reconstituted in water, these dried tomatoes make the best traditional sauce of all.

If good fresh tomatoes are available to you, use the same weight as that given for the canned tomatoes in the recipe and prepare as directed in the Quick Tomato Sauce. With this slow-cooked sauce, however, I recommend you do take the trouble to remove the seeds.

Remember that a tomato, while classified as a fruit, is still not like a peach. If you find the flavor of your tomatoes too sharp, do *not* add sugar, as you are often counseled to do, unless you are trying to achieve a specific taste. Instead, add two or three times the amount of onion called for in the recipe—but cook it first, if not adding at the beginning. You will be surprised at how sweet your tomato sauce will become from the natural sugar in the onions, and no one will be able to guess that you have a lot of onions in it. Somehow, added sugar in tomatoes can always be identified and often imparts an unpleasant taste. The onions, on the other hand, blend and integrate so well in this slow cooking that they cannot be tasted as such. The whole sauce tastes just wonderful. Use it on baked pasta or on big, stubby boiled pasta.

4 tablespoons extra virgin olive oil

1 large yellow onion, finely chopped

3 cloves garlic, finely chopped

2 1-pound, 12-ounce cans tomatoes, seeded and coarsely chopped

1 cup water

1 cup red wine

4 tablespoons tomato paste

1 sprig fresh oregano, or 1 teaspoon dried

Salt and pepper to taste

Place the oil and onion in a large, heavy pan over medium-high heat. Cook until the onion is soft and transparent. Add the garlic and cook until golden. Add all other ingredients. Lower heat, and simmer uncovered for 3 hours, stirring occasionally.

Salsa al Pomodoro
(Quick Tomato Sauce)
MAKES 2 GENEROUS QUARTS

This is a fresh-tasting, almost tart sauce that is excellent for pasta. It is also know as *Salsa alla Marinara* (Sailor Sauce). The same weight of fresh tomatoes may be used, and if they are sun-ripened and naturally sweet as they should be, the taste of the sauce will benefit greatly. Core and peel them before use.

However, unless the fresh tomatoes are truly fine, you are better off using good canned ones. Immature fresh tomatoes without well-developed fruit sugars will do nothing to improve this sauce and will more likely detract from its flavor.

1 large yellow onion, finely chopped
½ cup extra virgin olive oil
2 cloves garlic, finely chopped
2 1-pound, 12-ounce cans tomatoes, finely chopped
1 sprig fresh oregano, or 1½ teaspoons dried
4 leaves fresh basil, or 1½ teaspoons dried
Salt and pepper to taste
Pinch of crushed red pepper flakes (optional)

Place the onion and oil in a large, heavy pan over medium-high heat. Cook until the onion is soft and transparent Add the garlic and cook about 3 minutes more; add all other ingredients and continue to cook about 15 minutes, stirring occasionally. (The red pepper flakes produce a more profound taste.)

The fast cooking will help to reduce the sauce and make it thick, but be careful that it does not burn on the bottom.

Note: The same base can be used in making fish stew, by adding $\frac{1}{3}$ cup or more of white or red wine before cooking, and then adding the fish and shellfish just minutes before serving.

Pesto
(Pounded Herb Sauce)

SERVES 4

Traditional pesto from Genoa is delicious alone or as a topping for pasta. It can also be used as a decorative dressing for sliced hard-boiled eggs served as an appetizer; as a sauce for grilled meats or fish; as a sauce for sun-ripened sliced fresh tomatoes; in salads, in omelettes, and in whichever other ways an adventurous taste exploration would elect. Pesto is also sometimes made with fresh parsley (Italian parsley is the best) if basil is not available. The sauce was originally made by hand in a mortar and pestle, but a food processor does an adequate job; a blender is less satisfactory because you may have to add the oil too soon.

Fresh pesto should be used immediately. However, you can take advantage of basil season by making pesto in quantity and preserving it for future use. Just boil and sterilize a Mason jar. Fill it with pesto, up to 1 inch empty below the top of the jar. Cover the surface of the sauce with a generous $1/2$-inch layer of olive oil, to keep air from coming into contact with the sauce. Place in the refrigerator. *Do not freeze!* Pesto stored this way can be kept for months and may even improve with age. To use, scoop out the desired amount, bring to room temperature, stir well and add olive oil as needed. Be sure to replenish the fresh olive oil on the surface of the pesto still in the jar and promptly return the remaining supply to the refrigerator.

1 cup tightly packed fresh basil leaves

1 large clove garlic

1 heaping tablespoon freshly grated Parmesan cheese

1 tablespoon freshly grated Romano cheese

1 teaspoon pine nuts or walnuts

⅔ cup extra virgin olive oil (adjust less or more, depending on desired thickness of pesto)

Salt and pepper to taste

Put all ingredients, except the oil, in the food processor, taking pains to extract maximum juice and flavor from each of them. When the other ingredients are well blended into a paste, add the oil gradually, mixing constantly, until the sauce has reached the consistency desired. Season with salt and pepper.

Salsa Bolognese (or Ragù)

(Bolognese Meat Sauce)

MAKES ABOUT 2 1/2 CUPS

In America this is the most popular and best known of the famous Italian Ragù (meaning literally "stew") meat sauces. While purists know that the Ragù starts with a solid piece of meat, hand-cut with a knife or even snipped with kitchen scissors into tiny morsels, ground meat is used here for convenience. After cooking for a long time in the sauce, one can hardly tell the difference in how the meat was cut up. Try it both ways, with ground or hand-cut meat, and adopt the result you like best.

2 ounces Prosciutto di Parma fat or pancetta, finely chopped (about ¼ cup)

1 yellow onion, finely chopped

1 carrot, finely chopped

1 tender yellow stalk celery, including leaves, finely chopped

¾ pound ground round beef

½ whole clove (broken in half)

1 cup red wine

½ cup cream

1 teaspoon salt

¼ teaspoon pepper

1 cup finely chopped fresh or canned tomatoes, including juice

Put the prosciutto fat in a heavy pan and cook over medium heat until it melts. Add onion, carrot, and celery. When the mixture becomes a light golden color, add the meat, breaking it up with a fork, and cook, stirring frequently, until it just loses its pink color. Add the clove and red wine. Cook until the wine evaporates, about 10 to 15 minutes. Add the cream and lower the heat; cook gently until the cream practically disappears, then add the salt and pepper. Add the tomatoes and cook gently for about 2 hours, stirring occasionally.

The result should be a thick and lovely mass resembling a purée. This can be used as a sauce on tagliatelle or other pasta. It will keep in the refrigerator for 4 to 5 days, and it also freezes and holds well.

Balsamella
(Béchamel or White Sauce)

MAKES 1 PINT

This is a simple and reliable basic white sauce, widely useful in general cooking as well as in pasta. Known as béchamel in French cooking, the sauce actually originated as balsamella in Italy long before the sixteenth century, when Catherine de Médicis brought it to France.

Learning to make a really good balsamella sauce combines principles of cooking with many other valuable applications. Infusing milk with herbs and spices before using it in almost any recipe will add a rich and subtle flavor to your dish. A good balsamella can turn simple ingredients into an elegant feast. Buon appetito!

2 cups milk

1 grating of nutmeg, slice of onion, clove of garlic, and/or bay leaf for flavoring (optional)

3 tablespoons unsalted butter

3 tablespoons all-purpose unbleached flour

Salt to taste

White pepper to taste

Heat the milk in a saucepan over low heat and infuse it with any or all of the optional flavorings (or none, if you want a very bland-tasting sauce) by simply dropping them in the milk. Do not let the milk boil. Keep it hot.

In another saucepan melt the butter over medium heat; when it is melted and bubbling, add the flour all at once, stirring constantly with a whisk. Let the mixture cook for a couple of minutes, but don't let it burn or scorch. Take it off the heat for a moment and then add the hot milk, straining the milk through a small sieve. Add the salt and white pepper. Put the sauce back on the heat. Cook and stir constantly until it begins to boil. Then lower the heat, cook and stir until it is thick and glossy. Use it immediately.

Note: If you do not wish to use this sauce right away, butter a piece of parchment or waxed paper and push it right down against the surface of the sauce, pressing the paper tightly against the sides of the pan to keep all the air off the surface. You can store the sauce like this for several days in the refrigerator, and it will not "skin over" because it has been protected from the air. When you are ready to use it, simply remove the paper, place the sauce on the heat, and stir it until it is hot and glossy.

You can also make the sauce thinner or thicker by simply adding more or less of the liquid and solid ingredients. If the sauce is too thick, add a little hot milk and mix well, returning it to the heat for a bit, if necessary. If the sauce is too thin, cook it longer over low heat, being careful not to let it scorch.

Dry Pasta
(Pastasciutta)

Spaghetti Aglio e Olio
(Spaghetti with Garlic and Olive Oil)
SERVES 4 TO 6

This is a famous, simple pasta which many Italians call their favorite. Some say they eat it when they feel sad because it makes them feel happy again. Well, garlic is supposed to have curative powers. Suggested wines: Barbera or Gattinara

½ cup extra virgin olive oil
4 large cloves garlic, finely chopped
1 pound fresh or dried spaghetti
½ cup finely chopped fresh Italian
  parsley
Pinch of crushed red pepper flakes
  (optional)
Freshly ground or cracked black
  pepper

Place the oil and garlic in a skillet over medium heat and cook until garlic is light golden in color.

Cook the pasta al dente (see pages 28–29), and drain well. Transfer it to a heated serving bowl.

Add the parsley to the oil and garlic. Pour the mixture on the pasta, add the pepper flakes, and mix well. Sprinkle on the freshly ground or cracked black pepper and serve very hot. No cheese on this dish, please!

Spaghetti alla Carrettiera
(Spaghetti Coachman-Style)
SERVES 3 OR 4

This is another version of pasta with garlic, this time with the salty cheese, pecorino, used as a daily staple by people who need all the energy they can possibly generate.

Suggested wines: Barbera or Gattinara

3 large cloves garlic, finely chopped

¼ cup extra virgin olive oil

**1 generous cup chopped fresh
  Italian parsley**

**Generous pinch of crushed red
  pepper flakes**

Salt and pepper to taste

12 ounces fresh or dried spaghetti

**½ cup freshly grated pecorino
  cheese**

Gently brown the garlic in the oil, being careful not to burn it. Add the parsley, pepper flakes, and salt and pepper.

Cook the pasta al dente (see pages 28–29), and drain well. Add it to the garlic and oil mixture. Toss well. Add the cheese, toss again, and serve while very hot.

Fettuccine al Burro

(Thin Ribbon Pasta with Butter)

SERVES 4 TO 6

This is the very simple way many northern Italians prefer to enjoy their pasta.
Suggested wines: Alcamo or Soave

¾ cup unsalted butter
1 pound fresh fettuccine
½ cup freshly grated Parmesan
   cheese plus additional for passing
Freshly ground black pepper

Place the butter in a warm serving dish and allow it to become very soft.

Cook the pasta al dente (see pages 28–29), and drain well. Immediately transfer pasta to the dish of butter, and toss gently. Add cheese and toss gently again. Grind on the pepper. Serve at once, while hot! Pass the additional cheese at the table.

Fettuccine al Burro e Pinoli

(Thin Ribbon Pasta with Butter and Pine Nuts)

SERVES 4 TO 6

Be sure to keep an eye on the pine nuts as they toast in the skillet, because they can burn very quickly.
Suggested wines: Alcamo or Soave

5 tablespoons pine nuts
¾ cup unsalted butter
1 pound fresh fettuccine
½ cup freshly grated Parmesan
  cheese plus additional for passing
Freshly ground black pepper

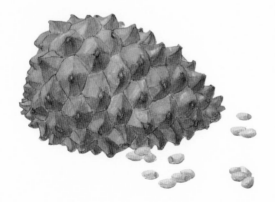

Gently brown the pine nuts in a heavy skillet over low heat, using no butter or oil and stirring continuously. When golden in color, immediately remove them from the heat and set aside.

Place the butter in a warm serving dish and allow it to become very soft.

Cook the pasta al dente (see pages 28–29), and drain well. Immediately transfer pasta to the dish of butter, and toss gently. Add the cheese and pine nuts, and toss gently again. Top with the pepper and serve immediately. Pass the additional cheese at the table. A delicious dish!

Tagliatelle alla Bolognese

(Thin Ribbon Pasta with Bologna-Style Sauce)

SERVES 4

This classic pasta from Bologna, considered by many to be the food capital of northern Italy, is best eaten in its home town, but you can achieve delicious results here if you don't oversauce it. Suggested wines: Arneis or Lambrusco

2½ cups Salsa Bolognese (Bolognese Meat Sauce, see page 49)
12 ounces or more fresh tagliatelle
½ cup or more freshly grated Parmesan cheese

Heat the sauce and keep it hot.

Cook the pasta al dente (see pages 28–29), and drain well. Return it to the cooking pot, add a little of the sauce, and mix thoroughly. Serve on a heated plate with a ladleful of sauce on top. Pass the cheese at the table.

Chiocciole al Mascarpone e Noci

(Small Pasta with Mascarpone and Walnuts)

SERVES 6

This is an elegant first-course pasta that should be eaten in small amounts. It is one of the many wonderful Italian pasta dishes that is still relatively unfamiliar in America.

Suggested wines: Alcamo Bianco or Rosato del Salento

1½ tablespoons unsalted butter

6 to 8 ounces mascarpone cheese

12 ounces dried 1-inch-size "shell" pasta

3 tablespoons freshly grated Parmesan cheese plus additional for passing

2 to 3 ounces walnut meats, coarsely chopped, plus additional larger pieces for garnish

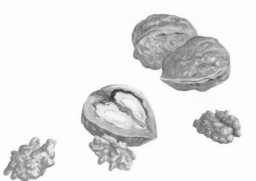

Melt the butter over low heat in a heatproof serving dish. Add the mascarpone and melt it slowly. Do not let it boil.

Cook the pasta al dente (see pages 28–29). Drain it, leaving a few spoonfuls of water in it. Add the pasta to the cheese and butter mixture and stir it all around. Add the Parmesan and the walnuts and mix again. Serve hot, garnished with the larger walnut pieces, and pass the additional Parmesan at the table.

Note: You may have trouble finding mascarpone. If you are offered torta, which is mascarpone layered with sweet Gorgonzola, be sure to accept it, because it is delicious in this dish, even though it has a slightly different flavor.

Penne al Salmone

("Pen" Macaroni with Smoked Salmon)

SERVES 6

If you're fond of smoked salmon, this unusual pasta recipe makes a delightful first course or a nice brunch dish. Since the smoked salmon is chopped for the sauce, you may be able to save by buying scraps or trimmings at less cost than the whole slices.

Suggested wines: Orvieto or Pinot Grigio

3 tablespoons unsalted butter

1 cup heavy cream

3 ounces best-cure smoked salmon (mildly salted and smoked), finely chopped

1 tablespoon finely chopped shallot

Juice of ½ large lemon

2 ounces Scotch whisky

Salt to taste

White pepper to taste

12 ounces dried penne

Freshly ground black pepper

Place the butter in a large frying pan over low heat. When it is melted, add the cream and reduce it by one third, about 5 minutes. Add the salmon and shallot and cook for about 2 minutes. Add the lemon juice and mix well. Add the whisky and cook long enough to let the alcohol evaporate, about 2 minutes. Season with salt and white pepper. Mix well.

Cook the pasta *very* al dente (see pages 28–29), and drain well. Add the well-dried pasta to the salmon mixture in the large frying pan. Gently mix so that the pasta is well coated. The sauce will finish cooking the pasta. Test for doneness. If the sauce is too dry, add some more cream. It should be very smooth and creamy, but the pasta should not swim in it. Freshly ground black pepper atop each serving "finishes" this dish.

Pasta Ericina

(Pasta as Made in Erice, Sicily)

SERVES 3 TO 4

Erice is perched on top of a mountain high above the city of Trapani on the southwest coast of Sicily. It is one of the most beautiful sites in Italy, and with just a touch of imagination on a very clear day you can see the north coast of Africa from this picturesque ancient hill town. The fresh Erice sauce can be used at room temperature or it can be very gently heated and served on hot or cold string beans or as a condiment for salmon or chicken. It should not be boiled or cooked. Sometimes I eat a cup or two of this delicious sauce as a snack, especially on hot days.
Suggested wines: Cirò Rosato or Corvo Rosso

1½ pounds fresh tomatoes, cored and peeled, or 1 pound 12 ounces canned

3 tablespoons extra virgin olive oil

Salt and pepper to taste

6 leaves fresh basil, chopped, or 1 teaspoon dried

½ pound fresh fettuccine or dried spaghetti or penne

⅓ cup finely chopped fresh Italian parsley

2 cloves garlic, finely chopped

Chop the tomatoes finely, transfer to a mixing bowl, and add a little oil. Add the salt, pepper, and basil. Let the mixture stand at room temperature for at least 1 hour to blend well.

Cook the pasta al dente (see pages 28–29), and drain well. Return it to the cooking pot, add some of the tomato sauce, mix well, and then add the rest. Transfer the pasta to a heated serving dish and top with the chopped parsley. Sprinkle on the garlic and serve.

Pasta all Sciacquina

(Pasta Washerwoman-Style)

SERVES 4

This pasta with its humble name is actually quite elegant and fit for a king. The cream, prosciutto, and best imported Parmesan are not inexpensive these days, but they combine here to achieve an absolutely irresistible result. Fettuccine, linguine, and penne are also good choices for this dish. Suggested wines: Cabernet Sauvignon or Chianti Riserva

2½ cups Salsa al Pomodoro (Quick Tomato Sauce, see page 47)

½ cup heavy cream

¼ pound Prosciutto di Parma, finely chopped

Salt and pepper to taste

12 ounces fresh spaghetti, or other long pasta

⅓ cup finely chopped fresh Italian parsley

Freshly grated Parmesan cheese for passing

Purée the prepared tomato sauce and add the heavy cream and prosciutto. Heat gently for about 10 minutes. Add the salt and pepper.

Cook the pasta al dente (see pages 28–29), and drain well. Transfer the pasta to a heated serving dish. Add some sauce and toss. Add more sauce and then sprinkle on the parsley. Finally, sprinkle the cheese over each portion and serve.

Trenette al Pesto

(Pasta with Pesto Sauce)

SERVES 6

This is always a favorite. The pesto's beautiful green color, its heady aroma, and its exquisite flavor add up to a real taste treat. Followed by a breaded veal cutlet, a green salad, and some fresh fruit with cheese, this can be a memorable meal.

Suggested wines: Barbera or Chianti Riserva

**1 cup Pesto (Pounded Herb Sauce,
  see page 48)**
1 pound trenette pasta
¼ cup extra virgin olive oil
Salt and pepper to taste
**½ cup freshly grated Parmesan
  cheese**

Bring the Pesto to room temperature.

Cook the pasta al dente (see pages 28–29). Drain, but reserve about ¾ cup of the water to dilute the pesto a bit. Place the pasta in a heated bowl. Add the oil and toss well. Dilute the Pesto with the pasta water, add the sauce to the bowl, and toss again. Add the salt and pepper. Pass the cheese at the table.

Maccheroni ai Quattro Formaggi

(Macaroni with Four Cheeses)

SERVES 6

This is a rich and luxurious pasta, due to the *abbondanza* (abundance) of beautiful cheeses used in the sauce. It makes an important first course for a special-occasion menu. Be sure to follow it with a light entrée, such as veal scallopini, squab, rack of lamb, or game.
Suggested wines: Montepulciano d'Abruzzo or Barolo

4 ounces unsalted butter
½ cup heavy cream
⅓ cup shredded Gorgonzola cheese
⅓ cup shredded fontina cheese
⅓ cup shredded Taleggio cheese
1 pound of any dried macaroni, such as rigatoni, penne, chiocciole, or other fancy shape
Salt and pepper to taste
½ cup freshly grated Parmesan cheese

Heat the butter and cream in a large saucepan over medium-low heat, being careful to keep it from boiling. Remove the rind from the three soft cheeses and discard them. Shred the cheeses and add to the cream and butter, whisking gently. Maintain the heat until they melt, keeping the sauce well whisked and blended. Remove from the heat and set aside.

Cook the pasta al dente (see pages 28–29), and drain well. Transfer the pasta to a heated bowl. Pour over the thick melted cheese sauce and toss well. Add salt and pepper.

Serve this dish piping hot, passing the Parmesan at the table.

Fettuccine alla Romana

(Ribbon Pasta with Cream, Butter, and Cheese)

SERVES 6

This pasta has become popularly known as "Fettuccine Alfredo" after the Alfredo Restaurant in Rome. Alfredo "introduced" this dish to America at the 1939 World's Fair in New York, where he complained that he needed water from the aqueducts in Rome to make the dish really perfect. Suggested wines: Frascati or Soave

¾ cup unsalted butter, at room temperature
1½ cups heavy cream
1 cup freshly grated Parmigiano-Reggiano cheese plus additional for passing
1 pound fresh fettuccine
Grating of fresh nutmeg, or a generous pinch of dried
Freshly ground black or white pepper

Place the butter in a large, heavy frying pan or similar vessel and put it in a warm place, even over very low heat, to melt but not cook.

Bring the cream to room temperature or warmer, and keep it handy.

Cook the pasta al dente (see pages 28–29), and quickly drain it, leaving it slightly wet. Immediately put the drained pasta into the frying pan with the butter and toss all around to coat the pasta well. Add the cream and grated cheese and gently toss again. Add the nutmeg and pepper and serve the pasta, which should be eaten immediately. Pass the additional cheese at the table.

Note: If the pasta looks a little too wet, don't worry. As the pasta sits in the dish, it absorbs quite a bit of the liquid. If the pasta looks perfectly creamy when you first serve it, it may become dry on the plate. Just to be sure, you may want to serve some additional soft unsalted butter along with additional cheese.

Also, you can partially whip the cream for the sauce so that it resembles a genuine "double cream" such as you would find in England. This increases the volume of the cream, but it also makes it lighter and more airy. It is a good trick, and you should try it at least once. Another name for the dish in Italy is *Tagliatelle alla Panna* (*panna* meaning "cream").

The measurements given in this recipe are only a guide. I have never really measured when making this dish personally and I would find it offensive to have to do so. The dish you will get is the result of judgment refined by experience and taste.

Linguine alle Vongole

(Pasta with Clams)

SERVES 4

This is a deservedly popular dish. It is quick and easy to make, at least with canned clams, which are available most everywhere. It can make a satisfying meal along with a green salad, a piece of fruit, and some good coffee.

Suggested wines: Pinot Bianco or Verdicchio

3 pounds small clams in their shells, or 2 7-ounce cans of chopped clams in their juice

⅓ cup extra virgin olive oil

2 or 3 large cloves garlic, finely chopped

Salt to taste

Plenty of freshly ground black pepper

Generous pinch of crushed red pepper flakes, or ⅓ cup heavy cream (optional)

2 tablespoons chopped fresh Italian parsley

1 pound linguine, spaghetti, or similar long-shaped pasta

Wash the clams shells well, scrubbing them with a brush to remove the sand and debris. Place them in a large frying pan with 1 tablespoon of the oil. Cover the pan and cook on high heat until the shells open wide. You may serve the clams in their shells, or remove them and discard the shells at this point. Either way, set aside. Then, strain the pan juices through a fine sieve to eliminate additional bits of shell and sand. Reserve the liquid. (If using canned clams, strain and reserve juice and clams, separated.)

Put the rest of the oil and the garlic in a frying pan over medium heat. Brown well but do not burn. Add the clam juice, salt and pepper, and either the red pepper flakes or cream. Add the parsley and clams. Remove from heat; set aside.

Cook the pasta al dente (see pages 28–29), and drain well. Transfer the pasta to a heated bowl. Pour the hot clam sauce over it (reheat the sauce first, if necessary) and mix well. Serve at once. Do *not* serve this dish with cheese.

Pasta alla Norma

(Pasta with Fried Eggplant)

SERVES 4 TO 6

This pasta is one of the gems in the crown of Sicilian cooking. Eaten outdoors with a soft Mediterranean breeze blowing, it will transport you to temporary heaven. The dish is known variously as *Pasta con Melanzane* (eggplant), *Pasta alla Norma* (the opera), or *Pasta alla Bellini* (after the great Sicilian composer who wrote the opera).

Suggested wines: Regaleali Rosso or Corvo Rosso

1 large, plump fresh eggplant

½ cup extra virgin olive oil

Salt to taste

Freshly ground black pepper

1 pound spaghetti or rigatoni or penne

1 quart Salsa al Pomodoro (Quick Tomato Sauce, see page 47)

About 20 large leaves fresh basil, chopped medium-fine

½ cup freshly grated ricotta salata or pecorino cheese

Cut the eggplant lengthwise into ¼-inch-thick slices. Do not remove the skin. (If the eggplant is truly fresh, there is no need to salt and "leach" it, because the juice will not be bitter.) Heat the oil in a frying pan, add the eggplant slices, and fry. Or, to conserve oil, you can liberally brush the eggplant slices with some oil and broil them. After the slices are nicely browned on both sides, transfer them to a dish lined with paper towels. Sprinkle with salt and pepper, and set aside.

Cook the pasta al dente (see pages 28–29), and drain well. Transfer the pasta to a heated bowl. Add a little of the sauce and toss. Serve on heated plates. Spoon a good amount of sauce on top of each portion and carefully lay 1 or 2 slices of fried eggplant on top of or alongside the sauce. Throw about 1 teaspoon of chopped fresh basil on top of each serving and pass the cheese at the table.

Bucatini all'Amatriciana

(Macaroni with Pancetta and Tomato)

SERVES 6

This dish comes from the town of Amatrice on the east coast of Italy by the Adriatic Sea. It has been adopted by the Romans, however, who have made the dish their own by adding some hot red pepper flakes, and also by sometimes using smaller cuts of pasta, such as spaghetti. Try the dish with and without the pepper flakes, and with larger and smaller pastas, and choose the version you like best. Suggested wines: Barbaresco or Vino Nobile di Montepulciano

2 tablespoons extra virgin olive oil

6 ounces pancetta, diced very small or thinly sliced (about 10 tablespoons)

1 small yellow onion, finely chopped

5 or 6 small fresh or canned tomatoes, peeled, seeded, and diced

Salt to taste

Freshly ground black pepper

1 pound bucatini or perciatelle

Generous pinch of crushed red pepper flakes

½ cup freshly grated pecorino cheese plus additional for passing

Heat the oil in a frying pan. Add the pancetta and onion and cook until light gold in color. Add the chopped tomatoes and cook gently, but do not let them get too soft. The pieces should remain intact. Taste and season with the salt and pepper.

Cook the pasta al dente (see pages 28–29), and drain well. Place the pasta in a heated bowl. Add the sauce and toss well. Adjust for salt and pepper, and then add the pepper flakes and cheese. Toss once more and serve hot, passing the additional cheese at the table.

Spaghetti alla Carbonara

(Spaghetti Coal Vendors–Style)

SERVES 4 TO 6

Some say this is a relatively new pasta recipe, originating in Rome after World War II when the Allied troops restored the city's supplies of eggs and bacon. Others say the dish has been used around the Sicilian coal mines since ancient times. I subscribe to the latter belief.

If you offer a simple antipasto (such as tuna fish in olive oil, Italian olives, celery, and mildly hot peperoncini), accompany the Spaghetti alla Carbonara with a nice big spinach salad, and follow with fresh fruit in season, you will serve a delicious meal with almost no labor at all.

Suggested wines: Aglianico or Montepulciano d'Abruzzo

2 tablespoons extra virgin olive oil
4 cloves garlic, slightly crushed
⅓ to ½ pound pancetta, sliced ⅛ inch thick and coarsely chopped
Generous ¼ cup dry white wine
4 large eggs, slightly beaten
Generous amount freshly ground black pepper
½ cup or more freshly grated Romano, Parmesan, or both, plus additional for passing
Salt to taste
1 pound spaghetti

Put the oil and garlic in a frying pan and cook over medium heat until the garlic is golden. Discard the garlic. Add the pancetta to the pan and cook until it is a light golden color. Do not let it burn. Add the wine and let the mixture boil for 3 or 4 minutes. Remove the pan from the heat and set aside.

In the bowl from which you will serve the pasta, place the beaten eggs, black pepper, salt and cheese. Mix together well with a fork, so that the ingredients are well blended. Set the bowl aside in a warm spot—not in a hot spot like the oven, or you will cook the eggs.

Cook the pasta al dente (see pages 28–29), and drain, leaving it quite wet. Add the pasta to the eggs in the bowl, stirring vigorously all the while so that the eggs cover the hot pasta without scrambling. In the meantime, reheat the pancetta until it is piping hot. Add it to the pasta mixture and toss well again. Serve immediately, passing the additional cheese at the table.

Editor's note: When preparing this dish, it is imperative that you use only the highest quality salmonella-free eggs.

Bigoli all'Anitra

(Venetian Wheat Pasta with Poached Duck)

SERVES 8

This is an unusual dish—though not in Venice—that you will really enjoy. The name *bigoli* comes from the contraption called a *bigolaro*, which produces the round thick shape.

Suggested wines: This dish is good with either red or white wine. I prefer a red wine such as Merlot or a Barbera, or a nice white such as a Pinot Grigio from the Veneto region near Venice.

4-pound duckling, cleaned and ready to cook (reserve the duck liver)
1 large yellow onion, coarsely chopped
1 stalk celery, coarsely chopped
1 large carrot, coarsely chopped
Salt to taste
6 to 8 tablespoons unsalted butter
1 large onion, finely chopped
1 large carrot, diced small
1 stalk celery, finely chopped
4 fresh sage leaves, chopped, or 2 teaspoons dried
1 duck liver, cut into 1-inch pieces
Poached duck meat, diced
Salt and pepper to taste
1 pound bigoli whole-wheat pasta
⅔ cup freshly grated Parmesan cheese

Put the duckling, onion, celery, and carrot into a stockpot. Cover with cold water half again as high as the duck. Add the salt. Bring to a gentle simmer. Skim the fat and scum from the surface of the water from time to time. Cook until the duck is tender, about 1 to 1½ hours.

When the duck is done, remove the carcass and skin it. (Save the skin and fry it in a little butter. When crisp, it is delicious added to a salad or just eaten by itself.) Remove the duck meat in small chucks. Set aside to cool; then dice. Strain the broth and degrease it. Discard the vegetables and reserve the broth.

To make the sauce, melt the butter in a frying pan. Add the onion, carrot, and celery and cook until golden. Add the sage and stir well. Add the duck liver (add more duck livers if you can get extras) and cook for about 3 minutes. Then add the diced duck meat and salt and pepper. Cook until everything is hot.

Cook the pasta al dente (see pages 28–29) in the reserved duck broth. Drain the pasta, again reserving the duck broth for another use. Add the sauce to the drained pasta and mix well. Sprinkle on half of the cheese and serve hot. Pass the remaining cheese at the

Paglia e Fieno

(Straw and Hay Pasta)

SERVES 4 TO 6

This is one of the times that I believe spinach pasta is justified. The color contrast in this dish is lovely and the flavor is so good that it puts the recipe in a class by itself. One can easily see how its name came about. The charm wore thin, however, when I was researching the origin of the recipe to check its authenticity. In true Italian fashion, I found at least five "proper" ways to prepare this dish, each one so different from the other that it is impossible to see how they can all refer to the same pasta. But at least they all do agree on its colors.

The making of spinach pasta is described on pages 22–23, or you can buy it dried. Whether you use fresh or dried pasta, remember that spinach pasta cooks faster than the plain kind, so put the plain pasta in the water for about a minute before you add the spinach pasta in order to equalize cooking times.

Suggested wines: Pinot Bianco or Verdicchio

4 tablespoons unsalted butter

1 yellow onion, finely diced

8 ounces boiled ham, or 5 ounces Prosciutto di Parma, shredded

⅔ cup fresh or frozen tiny peas

1 cup heavy cream

½ pound plain tagliarini (tagliolini)

½ pound green spinach tagliarini (see pages 22-23)

Salt and pepper to taste

2 generous gratings fresh nutmeg

¾ cup freshly grated Parmesan cheese plus additional for passing

Melt the butter in a heavy frying pan over medium-low heat. Add the onion and cook until transparent. Add the ham and cook for about 5 minutes. Add the peas and stir well for about 1 minute. Add the cream and cook 5 more minutes to allow the cream to thicken a little. Add the salt, pepper, and nutmeg.

Cook the pasta al dente (see pages 28–29), and drain well. Put the pasta in a heated bowl. Add half the sauce and half the cheese and mix very well. Top with the remaining sauce and cheese. Pass more cheese at the table if you wish.

Spaghetti alla Puttanesca

(Hookers' Pasta)

SERVES 4 OR 6

No one seems to know why this pasta was named after the ladies in the world's oldest profession. Perhaps the fact that it can be eaten cold explains it—they could cook, do some business, and have a tasty cold meal ready. I'm afraid I don't know, but the dish is quite good! It is best eaten hot. But at room temperature it could be a tasty meal on a hot day when you want a "do-ahead" dish. Suggested wines: Lacryma Christi del Vesuvio or Chianti Classico

2 or 3 tablespoons extra virgin olive oil

2 cloves garlic, minced

2 ounces or more calamata or Gaeta olives, pitted and coarsely chopped

1 teaspoon coarsely chopped capers

1 large fresh tomato, peeled and coarsely chopped

4 or 5 anchovy fillets, coarsely chopped

1 pound spaghetti

⅓ cup finely chopped fresh Italian parsley

Salt and pepper to taste

Place the oil and garlic in a frying pan over medium heat. When the garlic is golden, add the olives, capers, tomato, and anchovy fillets. Stir well and heat through for about 6 minutes.

Cook the pasta al dente (see pages 28–29), and drain well. Place the pasta in a heated bowl and add half the sauce. Toss well. Add the remaining sauce and sprinkle on the parsley, salt, and pepper. Serve hot. Please, no cheese with this dish.

Spaghetti alla Viareggina

(Spaghetti with Clams and Tomato)

SERVES 4 TO 6

This very popular dish from Viareggio in Tuscany is equally at home in Rome, Naples, and Sicily. It is often made with linguine and other long pastas. Even people who do not ordinarily care much for clams will eat this recipe with gusto. There is a very fresh quality about this pasta that makes you want to eat more, even though you may already be quite full. A nice small breaded veal cutlet just plain, with a splash of lemon juice, is a perfect follow-up.

Suggested wines: A nice young wine such as a Rosato del Salento or Verdicchio would be my choice with this pasta, whether or not I planned to have veal afterwards.

3 pounds small clams in their shells, or 2 7-ounce cans of chopped clams in their juice

⅓ cup olive oil

3 large cloves garlic, finely chopped

⅓ cup dry white wine

1 pound fresh tomatoes, peeled and chopped, or 14 ounces canned (about 2 cups)

Salt to taste

Plenty of freshly ground black pepper

Generous pinch of crushed red pepper flakes

1 pound spaghetti

⅓ cup chopped fresh Italian parsley

Wash and prepare clams (refer to instructions for Linguine alle Vongole, page 66).

Put the oil and garlic in a frying pan over medium heat. Brown well, but do not burn. Add the wine, tomatoes, clams, and their juice. Taste for salt and add more as needed. Cook over high heat for 2 minutes. Add black pepper and red pepper flakes and cook until the clams are done and the sauce is slightly thickened. Do not overcook the clams.

Cook the spaghetti al dente (see pages 28–29), and drain well. Place the pasta in a heated bowl. Add half the sauce and mix well. Top with the remaining sauce and sprinkle on the parsley. Please, no cheese with this dish.

Maccheroni con la Capuliata

(Macaroni with ground meat)

SERVES 4

Capuliata is Sicilian for "chopped beef," which is quite a treat for Sicilians. Because beef is not produced to any degree, their consumption runs more to fish, game, pork, kid, and chicken. This is a hearty dish, satisfying to both soul and body; it makes a wonderful one-dish supper.
Suggested wines: A robust red, such as Cabernet Sauvignon or Merlot.

¼ cup extra virgin olive oil

1 onion, finely chopped

1 large clove garlic, peeled and finely chopped

½ pound or a little more ground chuck or other beef

½ cup red wine

3 tablespoons chopped fresh Italian parsley

2 tablespoons chopped fresh basil leaves, or 3 tablespoons dried

1 pound fresh tomatoes, peeled and finely chopped, or 14 ounces canned (about 2 cups)

Salt and pepper to taste

Pinch of crushed red pepper flakes

12 ounces short, stubby-shaped dried pasta, such as penne or rigatoni

¾ cup grated provolone or caciocavallo cheese plus additional for passing

Place the oil and onion in a frying pan over medium heat and gently cook the onion until just soft. Add the garlic and cook until golden. Add the meat and cook, stirring to break up any lumps, until it just loses its redness. Add the wine and cook for about 10 minutes more. Add everything else except the pasta and cheese. Simmer the mixture for about 30 minutes.

Cook the pasta al dente (see pages 28–29), and drain well. Place the pasta in a bowl and mix it with half the sauce and half the cheese. Top with the rest of the sauce and cheese. Serve it very hot and pass the additional cheese at the table.

Note: In Sicily this dish is often prepared as described and, when completed, put into a well-oiled casserole. The top is liberally sprinkled with more cheese, and the dish is then baked in a preheated 400° oven for about 20 minutes. It is served very hot.

Rigatoni alla Donnafugata

("The Leopard's" Rigatoni)

SERVES 6

This is my own version of a very enjoyable pasta featured at the Fico D'India Restaurant in Palermo, Sicily. *Donnafugata* is the name given by Giuseppe di Lampedusa in his book, *The Leopard*, to the beloved country palace of Don Fabrizio, Prince of Salina.
Suggested wine: Barbera

½ pound veal shoulder

1 cup Brodo di Carne or Brodo di Scuro (Meat Broth, page 114, or Dark Meat Broth, page 115)

3 sprigs Italian parsley'

1 small carrot

1 bay leaf

¼ cup extra virgin olive oil

2 ounces pancetta, finely chopped

4 to 6 scallions, finely chopped

¼ pound Prosciutto di Parma, thinly sliced and cut into ½-inch pieces

14 fresh artichoke hearts, trimmed, blanched, and quartered, or 1 10-ounce package frozen artichoke hearts, quartered

3 to 4 tablespoons tomato paste

¼ cup or more dry marsala

Salt to taste

Freshly ground black pepper

¼ pound fresh porcini or other mushrooms, thinly sliced

1 cup fresh or frozen tiny peas

1½ cups heavy cream

1¼ pounds rigatoni

2 tablespoons unsalted butter

1 cup or more finely grated Parmigiano-Reggiano cheese

Cut the veal into 2 by 2-inch pieces. and cook it in the broth with the parsley, carrot, and bay leaf for 1 hour. Drain the meat, shred it, and set aside. Strain the broth and reserve it.

Heat the oil in a heavy frying pan over medium heat. Add the pancetta and cook until it is slightly colored. Add the scallions, prosciutto, veal, and artichoke hearts. Cook for about 7 or 8 minutes. Add the tomato paste, marsala, broth, salt, and pepper, and simmer for 7 or 8 minutes. Add the mushrooms and peas and simmer for 5 minutes. Add the cream and continue to cook until all ingredients are very hot.

Cook the pasta al dente (see pages 28–29), and drain well. Return it to the cooking pot, add the butter and quickly toss. Place the pasta in a bowl and top with sauce. Serve at once, passing the cheese at the table.

Pasta Arriminata

(Pasta with Broccoli "Stirred Around")

SERVES 6

This dish is representative of the ingenious flavors and textures of Sicilian cuisine, which is certainly the most complex of all the Italian regional cuisines and the most difficult to understand. However, if you simply let yourself enjoy the tastes without analyzing them, you will find this dish, along with so many other Sicilian dishes, a rewarding experience.

Suggested wine: Chardonnay

1 bunch broccoli, 1 head cauliflower, or a mixture of both, trimmed and cut into square pieces about 1½ by 1½ inches

⅓ cup extra virgin olive oil

1 large yellow onion, finely diced

3 anchovy fillets, chopped

½ cup seedless white raisins

⅓ cup pine nuts

Small pinch saffron

Salt to taste

Freshly ground black pepper

1 pound dried macaroni, such as rigatoni, penne, large shells, or large elbows

½ cup or more freshly grated pecorino cheese

Blanch the broccoli (and/or cauliflower) in boiling salted water until it is barely tender. Do not overcook. Drain, cool, and set aside.

Place the oil and onion in a frying pan over medium heat. Fry the onion until golden. Add the broccoli, anchovy fillets, raisins, pine nuts, saffron, salt, and pepper. Gently cook until the flavors are well blended, about 5 or 6 minutes.

Cook the pasta al dente (see pages 28–29) and drain, leaving about ¼ cup water in it. Add the sauce and stir well. Sprinkle on the cheese. Serve hot.

Note: Sometimes Sicilian cooks add 1 cup crushed tomatoes to the sauce during cooking. Also, the dish is sometimes baked in an oiled casserole at 400° for 20 minutes.

Minestra di Ditalini e Cavolfiore

(Ditalini Pasta with Cauliflower)

SERVES 6

My mother made this on cold, mournful days, and mostly, we ate it in silence, letting the heat from the pasta build up inside until we broke a little sweat. It was almost mystical. On a more practical level, leftovers are delicious as a cold soup eaten with intermittent bites of radishes and young stalks of celery. Suggested wines: Vermentino or Regaleali Rosso

1 large head cauliflower, trimmed of outer leaves

6 teaspoons salt

3 tablespoons extra virgin olive oil

1 large yellow onion, finely chopped

2 large cloves garlic, finely chopped

½ teaspoon or more crushed red pepper flakes (I like more)

½ teaspoon or more freshly ground black pepper

1 pound ditalini or similar short, stubby pasta

1 cup grated aged pecorino cheese

Cut the cauliflower, including the stem, into small pieces and wash them in cold water. Bring a stockpot of water and 4 teaspoons of the salt to a boil. Place the cauliflower in the boiling water and cook it for about 4 minutes; drain and transfer it to a dish or bowl, reserving the water for boiling the pasta. (This can all be done a few hours ahead.)

Heat about 1 tablespoon of the oil in a large sauté pan, add the onion, and sauté it until translucent, about 5 or 6 minutes. Add the garlic and sauté until fragrant, about 2 minutes. Add the pepper flakes, black pepper, and the remaining 2 teaspoons salt.

Bring the cauliflower water to a boil again, add the pasta, and stir well. Cook the pasta al dente (see pages 28–29). Drain it, discarding all but 1 ½ cups of the water, or reserving the remainder to use as a base for vegetable soup.

Add the pasta and about ⅓ cup of the reserved pasta water to the sauté pan with the onion mixture. Stir until the pasta is cooked a bit more and almost ready to eat, about 2 to 3 minutes, then add the cauliflower and stir well until it is very hot. Add a bit more of the remaining 1 cup and 3 tablespoons of pasta water. The dish should be very moist but not souplike.

Sprinkle with the cheese. Drizzle with the remaining 2 tablespoons of oil, or more as you like, and serve.

Pappardelle al Radicchio Saltato

(Pappardelle with Sautéed Radicchio)

SERVES 6

Pappardelle are 1-inch-wide, flat noodles as thin as fettuccine, usually made fresh and hand-cut. You may use similar noodles or even fettuccine, but I love to see these wide ribbons of pasta on the plate, and if you eat pasta for its own sake, the flavor really comes through. This is one of the simplest pasta dishes around, so I would follow it with grilled fish with lemon and rosemary, or baked chicken basted with balsamic vinegar. I do not use cheese, but if you must, use a small amount of grated Parmigiano-Reggiano. Suggested wines: Alcamo Bianco or Corvo Rosso

5 ounces, or more or less, pancetta, sliced ¼ inch thick and finely chopped

3 tablespoons extra virgin olive oil

2 large red onions, coarsely cut into ½-inch dice

2 heads radicchio di chioggia (round heads)

Sea salt to taste

Plenty of freshly ground black pepper

1½ pounds fresh pappardelle, or 1 pound dried

Put the pancetta into a heavy skillet over medium heat. When the fat melts, sauté the pancetta until it is light gold. Remove the pancetta and discard all the fat. Wipe the pan clean, add a tablespoon or so of the olive oil, and sauté the onions until soft with little scorch marks here and there. Set aside in a bowl.

Trim the radicchio and remove the old or soft outer leaves. Trim out some of the stem and discard it. Coarsely chop the radicchio into 1-inch pieces. Add the remaining 2 tablespoons of oil to the skillet and sauté the radicchio until it is tender, but not too soft. Combine all the sautéed ingredients and season with salt and pepper.

Cook the pasta until al dente (see pages 28–29), making sure the other ingredients are hot when the pasta is almost done. Drain the pasta, but leave about 2 to 3 tablespoons of water in it. Mix the pasta with the sautéed ingredients. Serve on heated plates.

Fusilli delle Madonie

(Fusilli Pasta with a Sauce of Fried Potatoes, Onion, Beef, Prosciutto, and Saffron)

SERVES 6

The Madonie, the austere mountain ranges in the northern/central region of Sicily, understandably has hearty food. You would think lamb would be the meat of choice in such a region, but, no, it is beef. This dish would be great to eat before conquering a very high mountain. It is also terrific on cold blustery days. Leftovers, gently heated, make a tasty and convenient snack sometime around midnight. Suggested wines: Cannonau di Sardegna or Barbaresco

3 tablespoons extra virgin olive oil

1 pound russet potatoes, peeled and cut into small dice

1 large yellow onion, cut into thin slices or diced

1 small celery heart, cut into small pieces

Generous pinch of chopped fresh Italian parsley

½ pound ground beef

4 ounces Prosciutto di Parma, thinly sliced and cut into ¼-inch pieces

Scant ½ teaspoon salt

¼ teaspoon or more freshly ground black pepper

Generous pinch of saffron

1 pound dried long or short fusilli

Put the oil in a large skillet over medium-low heat. Add the potatoes and sauté until they are light gold. Add the onion and sauté until it is soft and translucent. Add the celery and stir well. After about 3 minutes, add the parsley, ground beef, prosciutto, salt, pepper, and saffron and stir well. The mixture will be a bit dry, but do not worry, it will eventually moisten. If it doesn't, add a few drops of water and a bit more oil. Sauté the mixture on low heat until cooked and creamy, not dry, and stir often.

Cook the pasta al dente (see pages 28–29), and drain, leaving in some of the water. Mix the pasta and the sauce and serve very hot. No cheese on this dish, please!

Rigatoncini al Basilico e Panna

(Small Rigatoni with Basil and Cream)

SERVES 6

A dish of this pasta and a green salad make a great small meal. Or, in smaller portions, it is terrific as a first course when you want a meal with several dishes. It is rich and tasty. You can serve small amounts of meat or fowl to keep the meal from being too filling, and it is economical, too. If you make the sauce totally a day or two ahead, you could make Rigatoncini al Basilico e Panna for a buffet without much last-minute rush, except for cooking pasta. The flavors are special.

Suggested wines: Lacryma Christi del Vesuvio or Orvieto

3 ounces pancetta, sliced ¼ inch thick and cut into small dice

1 tablespoon extra virgin olive oil

5 ounces unsalted butter

2 cloves garlic, finely chopped

3 ounces brandy

1 cup heavy cream

1 large tomato, cored, peeled, and finely diced

About 1 teaspoon crushed red pepper flakes

Sea salt to taste

Freshly ground black pepper to taste

1 pound rigatoncini or similar stubby pasta

1 ¼ cups grated pecorino cheese plus additional for passing

Put the pancetta and oil in a sauté pan over medium heat and sauté until it is slightly crispy and golden. Drain any excess fat and then add the butter and garlic. Sauté the garlic until it is golden, about 2 minutes. Add the brandy. If you are using a gas flame, the fumes from the brandy will flame almost without help. If cooking on a electric stove, use a match to set fire to the brandy—but don't get burned! Add the cream, tomato, pepper flakes, salt, and pepper, and let everything simmer on medium heat for about 5 minutes. The cream mixture should be thick but still liquid enough to use as a sauce.

Cook the pasta al dente (see pages 28–29). Drain it, but be sure to save 4 to 6 tablespoons of the water to thin the sauce, if necessary. Toss the pasta with the sauce in the sauté pan or use a heated bowl. Serve on heated plates and top with the cheese. Pass the additional cheese at the table.

Tagliolini ai Gallinacci

(Tagliolini with Chanterelles)

SERVES 6

Chanterelle mushrooms are called *gallinacci* (big hens), or sometimes *gallinelli* (little hens), because of their plump, curvy caps and orangy golden color. Other mushrooms can be used, but this dish is beautiful with the colorful chanterelles peeking out here and there. The flavor is milky and nutty—perfect for fall or spring when *gallinacci* are in abundance. You can use most any pasta, but I like to use stringy ones, such as linguine, spaghetti, and long fusilli. Stubby pasta works well, too.
Suggested wines: Arneis or Chianti

4 tablespoons extra virgin olive oil

3 large cloves garlic, finely chopped

5 to 6 ounces chanterelle mushrooms, cleaned and cut into ½-inch dice

½ cup dry white wine

½ cup chicken stock

4 scallions, washed, trimmed, and sliced ½ inch long

3 tablespoons coarsely chopped fresh Italian parsley

Sea salt to taste

Plenty of freshly ground black pepper

1½ pounds fresh tagliolini, or 1 pound dry

Put the oil in a large sauté pan over medium heat. Add the garlic and mushrooms and sauté until the garlic is a deep golden color. Stop the garlic from cooking by adding the wine and stock. Reduce for about 10 minutes, so that the sauce is no longer liquid but is nicely moist. Add the scallions and parsley and combine well. Set aside the sauce.

Cook the pasta al dente (see pages 28–29), and drain, leaving about 2 to 3 tablespoons of water in it. Mix the pasta with the sautéed ingredients.

Serve immediately on heated plates.

Fusilli alla Carlo

(Fusilli as Carlo Makes It)

SERVES 6

I am a traditionalist and proud of it, but once, in the kitchen at Vivande Porta Via, dog-tired after working since early morning, I just started combining ingredients and came up with this dish for my lunch. Eight people spotted it and wanted it. Ecco, a dish was born. It is by far the most popular dish we regularly do on our menu.

Toast large amounts of pine nuts (see directions, below) and freeze them in small glass jars. They will keep for several months. You can also toast them in a 350° oven for about 10 to 12 minutes, although I do not like this method because I forget they are in there.

Suggested wines: Cirò Rosato or Aglianico

5 tablespoons pine nuts

3 ounces pancetta, sliced ¼ inch thick and cut into small dice

5 tablespoons extra virgin olive oil

5 ounces unsalted butter

5 ounces button mushrooms, sliced medium-thin

Sea salt to taste

Freshly ground black pepper to taste

1 large tomato, cored, peeled, and finely diced

1 cup heavy cream

1 pound fusilli

⅓ cup grated Parmigiano-Reggiano cheese

1 cup grated pecorino cheese plus additional for passing

Place a heavy 8-inch sauté pan over medium heat. In about 1½ minutes, add the pine nuts (but no fat) and immediately reduce the heat to low. Stir the pine nuts constantly so they toast evenly, for about 5 minutes. Watch carefully because they burn easily. When they are done, immediately pour them into a cool dish or bowl, which stops the cooking.

Put the pancetta and oil into a sauté pan and sauté until the pancetta is slightly crispy and golden. Drain any excess fat, then add the butter, mushrooms, salt, pepper, pine nuts, and tomato, and sauté for about 2 minutes. Add the cream and reduce for about 4 minutes. Stir in the Parmigiano-Reggiano. Keep warm over low heat.

Cook the pasta al dente (see pages 28–29), and drain, saving about 4 to 6 tablespoons of the water.

Toss the pasta with the sauce. If the sauce is too thick, add 1 or more tablespooons of the reserved pasta water. Serve on heated plates and top with the pecorino cheese, passing more at the table.

82

Fettuccine alla Giovanni

(John's Fettuccine with Smoked Sausage)

SERVES 6

John Hudson, one of Vivande Porta Via's chefs de cuisine in the early days, and I came up with this dish. We smoke our chickens, trout, turkey, oysters, and our own house-made sausages. One day we were hungry and wanted more than just the sausage, so we came up with this dish, which everyone loves, and we sell lots of it. Do not use heavy smoked sausage. Smoke your own in your barbecue, and be sure the sausages are the best. For my authentic recipe from Agrigento, Sicily, where my father was born, see my book, *The Food of Southern Italy*.

Suggested wines: Alcamo Bianco or Cannonau di Sardegna

4 to 5 links, about 1 or 1½ pounds lightly smoked sausage

4 tablespoons extra virgin olive oil

3 cloves garlic, finely chopped

Sea salt to taste

Freshly ground black pepper to taste (use lots)

1 cup dry white wine

1 tomato, cored, peeled, and finely chopped

1½ pounds fresh spinach or plain fettuccine, or 1 pound dry

1 small bunch (about 1 pound) spinach, washed and well trimmed

1 teaspoon crushed red pepper flakes or to taste

Roast the sausage on a baking rack over a roasting pan with sides in a preheated 375° oven for about 30 minutes. Or put the sausage into a large skillet and add about 1½ cups water.

Place a lid on the pan and simmer the sausages for about 15 minutes. Discard any water and continue to sauté the sausages until they are dark gold and done. In either case, cool the links and cut them into large chunks (about 6 pieces per link).

Place a large skillet over medium heat and add the sausage pieces, oil, garlic, and some salt and pepper. Sauté until the sausage is hot and the garlic is golden. Pour in the white wine to stop the garlic from cooking. Add the tomato, and continue to cook until most of the wine is evaporated, about 5 to 6 minutes.

Cook the pasta al dente (see pages 28–29) and drain, being sure that it is wet. Fill a large sauté pan with the spinach. Transfer the pasta to the sauté pan and toss well. This mixes everything and collapses the spinach just a little. Serve the hot pasta on heated plates, sprinkling the pepper flakes over the top.

Spaghetti con le Cozze

(Spaghetti with Mussels)

SERVES 6

When you can, use mussels harvested from icy cold water that are not too big and that smell like an ocean breeze. They will make this dish second to no other. Prince Edward Island mussels are good, as are those from Penn Cove, and of course there are some good green lip mussels from New Zealand, but they all must be small to be really tasty.

This is an elegant dish the way I serve it. There is less pasta in this dish than in others, on purpose. I make a necklace around the rim of the dish with the open shiny black oval mussels and then plop the pasta right in the middle of the plate and sprinkle on plenty of Italian parsley, not as garnish, but as part of the taste sensation. And there you have it. Pretty as a picture and irresistible.

Suggested wines: Chardonnay or Friuli-Venezia Giulia

3 pounds of mussels
4 tablespoons extra virgin olive oil
3 cloves garlic, finely chopped
Sea salt to taste
Freshly ground pepper to taste
1 cup dry white wine
1 cup Salsa al Pomodoro (Quick Tomato Sauce, see page 47)
14 ounces fresh spaghetti or fettuccine or 8 ounces dry
⅓ cup chopped fresh Italian parsley

Scrub the mussels with a vegetable brush, and pull off any "beard" they may have. Soak them in very cold water for about 30 minutes, shaking them often.

In a very large skillet, heat the oil over medium-low heat, add the garlic, some salt and pepper, and the mussels, well drained of their soaking water. Shake the pan vigorously, and add the wine. When the mussels begin to open, add the sauce and stir well. The liquid must be very hot, and the mussels should take about 2 minutes to cook. Do not overcook them, because they become like rubber bands.

Cook the pasta al dente (see pages 28–29) and drain, being sure that it is wet. (If using dry pasta, start cooking it before you cook the mussels.)

When the mussels are open and hot, quickly remove them from the pan with tongs and arrange them around the rim of the plates. Discard any mussels that do not open.

Meanwhile, the sauce remaining in the pan should be boiling vigorously. Add the pasta to the sauce and stir well. Place equal portions of pasta in the center of the plates, sprinkle heavily with the parsley, and serve immediately. Please, no cheese.

Fettuccine con Pomodori Scoppiati

(Fettuccine with "Bursted" Tomatoes)

SERVES 6

When Kevin Baker, my chef de cuisine at Vivande Ristorante, came back from a trip to Sicily, he cooked this dish for days, trying to get the flavors right (just like "over there") using our produce. It worked. *Scoppiato* means "burst" or "exploded," and of course this happens when you put tiny tomatoes into a hot pan.

Suggested wines: Merlot or Montepulciano d'Abruzzo

1 large red bell pepper, or a mixture of yellow and orange bell pepper

5 tablespoons extra virgin olive oil

2 large cloves garlic, well crushed

Sea salt to taste

Freshly ground black pepper

1 pound or more yellow and red cherry tomatoes, washed and stemmed

¼ cup coarsely chopped fresh Italian parsley

6 ounces imported provolone cheese, finely diced

1½ pounds fresh fettuccine, or 1 pound dry

1 teaspoon crushed red pepper flakes or more to taste

Wash the bell pepper. Hold it directly over a gas flame until it becomes almost black. When the skin is blistered all over, remove the pepper from the heat and let it cool uncovered on a plate. When cool, peel off the skin with a par-ing knife or your fingers, split it open, and scrape out the seeds. Do not wash it with water because it diminishes the flavor. (Little black spots are normal and desirable on fire-roasted peppers.) If you use an electric or gas broiler, cut the pepper into quarters and place the skin side as close to the heat source as possible. Proceed as directed. When the pepper is skinned, cut it into ½-inch dice.

Put the oil in a large skillet and place it over medium heat. Add the garlic and salt and pepper, and sauté until golden. Add the bell pepper and sauté until hot. Add the tomatoes and sauté until they soften a bit and start exploding, about 5 minutes or less.

Cook the pasta al dente (see pages 28–29), making sure the sauce is hot when the pasta is almost done. Add the parsley and provolone cheese to the sauce and stir. Drain the pasta, leaving it slightly wet. Add it to the pan of sauce and mix well. Serve the pasta on heated plates and sprinkle with the pepper flakes.

Fettuccine al Vodka

(Fettuccine with Vodka)

SERVES 6

I like this dish with fettuccine, but tagliolini are also good. Sometimes I love it with penne or rigatoncini, and once in a while I use squid-ink pasta. I consider this an elegant dish because of its appearance, but also because of the suave taste; it is sultry and sexy and, oh, so sophisticated. It is one of the all-time favorites at both my Vivande restaurants. Followed by a small piece of fish or fowl, a tiny salad, and some fresh fruit, you have quite a meal for making *la bella figura* (looking good). Suggested wines: Pinot Grigio or Arneis

3 ounces pancetta, sliced ¼ inch thick and cut into small dice

1 tablespoon extra virgin olive oil

Sea salt to taste

2 tomatoes, cored, peeled, and finely diced

1½ pounds fresh fettuccine, or 1 pound dry

1 bunch scallions, cleaned, washed, dried, and cut into 1-inch diagonal pieces (use both white and green parts)

⅓ cup vodka

1 cup grated Parmigiano-Reggiano cheese plus additional for passing

Coarsely ground black pepper

To make the sauce, put the pancetta and oil in a large skillet. Sauté over medium heat until the pancetta is gold and slightly crunchy. Add some salt. Remove from the heat and add the tomatoes.

Cook the pasta al dente (see pages 28–29), and drain, leaving a bit of water in it. Meanwhile, reheat the sauce, add the scallions, remove the pan from the heat source, and carefully add the vodka. Stir well, and let some of the alcohol evaporate, about 1½ minutes. *Never add the vodka while the sauce is on a heat source because it could flare up and startle or injure you.* Add the pasta and toss well.

Serve on heated plates, sprinkling on plenty of the cheese and black pepper. Pass the additional cheese at the table.

Penne alla Primavera

(Penne Pasta for Springtime)

SERVES 6

Nowadays, when there are no longer seasons, at least when it comes to buying ingredients such as produce, this name could be passé. But the spirit is there. The idea is to use as many different vegetables as you like, simply prepared and mixed in with pasta. This is an ideal dish for the vegan family or friends. You can use packaged pasta, which almost invariably is simply made with semolina and water. Be sure to read the ingredients listed on the package.

To make this dish low-calorie, substantially reduce the amount of oil and add lots more garlic and pepper. Kids love this dish and will eat loads of vegetables prepared this way. They especially like the shape of penne, but you can use fresh pasta such as tagliolini or fettuccine if you like.

Wine suggestions: Pinot Bianco or Valpolicella

1 pound or more red, green, or yellow bell peppers or a mixture of all three

5 tablespoons or more extra virgin olive oil

3 small zucchini, washed, trimmed, and cut into ¼-inch slices

6 ounces button or crimini mushrooms, brushed clean and chopped medium-coarse

3 large cloves garlic, finely chopped

2 large tomatoes (about 12 ounces), cored, peeled, and chopped medium-coarse

Sea salt to taste

1 pound penne or similar pasta

Freshly ground black pepper

Wash the bell peppers well. Dry and core them, and discard the seeds. Cut them into ¼-inch-wide slices. Put 2 tablespoons of the olive oil into a large skillet over medium heat and sauté the peppers until they are barely soft and have not begun to brown. Add the zucchini, and sauté for about 2 minutes. Add the mushrooms and garlic, and cook another 2 minutes, stirring frequently. Add the tomatoes and turn off the heat. Add some salt.

Cook the pasta al dente (see pages 28–29), and drain, leaving it wet. Heat the sauce, if it has cooled, mix in the pasta, and serve on heated plates. Sprinkle on lots of pepper and drizzle on the remaining 3 tablespoons of oil.

Fettuccine con Pumate e Gallinacci

(Fettuccine with Sundried Tomatoes and Chanterelles)

SERVES 6

Sundried tomatoes, all the rage these days, were first developed by the Italians as a way to preserve vine-ripened tomatoes for sauce-making during the harsh winter and early spring months.

Pumate is a special name given to sundried tomatoes in Liguria on the Italian Riviera. Nowadays, these incredibly tasty tomatoes, which cost a fortune, are made to remain soft but leathery, and are soaked in extra virgin olive oil to be eaten as a condiment more than as a sauce. If you buy local dried tomatoes, briefly boil them about 2 minutes and let them soak for another 10 minutes. Gently squeeze them dry and then marinate them in extra virgin olive oil for at least a couple of hours. Pumate combined with chanterelles can make the angels sing.

Suggested wines: Orvieto or Verdicchio

5 ounces unsalted butter

1 small yellow onion, finely chopped

Sea salt to taste

6 ounces pumate, or 4 ounces dehydrated tomatoes

8 ounces chanterelle mushrooms, cleaned and coarsely chopped

1 cup or a bit more heavy cream

1½ pounds fresh fettuccine, or 1 pound dried

Freshly ground black pepper

Put the butter in a large skillet over medium heat. When the butter melts, add the onion and salt. Sauté gently until the onion is translucent. Add the tomatoes, chopped into small pieces. Olive oil–packed tomatoes can be used without straining or pressing to remove the oil; the oil that clings just adds flavor. If you use dried ones, be sure not to disintegrate them by soaking or boiling them too long. Add the mushrooms and sauté until they are tender, about 5 minutes. Add the cream and reduce for about 3 or 4 minutes.

Cook the pasta al dente (see pages 28–29) and drain, leaving it slightly wet.

If you have made the sauce ahead, reheat it now. Add the cooked pasta and toss well. Serve on heated plates and top with plenty of pepper. No cheese, please.

Pappardelle con i Porcini

(Pappardelle with Porcini Mushrooms)

SERVES 6

If you can find fresh porcini mushrooms (*Boletus edulis*), use them to make this epicurean dish. Porcini are best in fall and winter when they can be harvested from forests where chestnut trees grow, although they may be hard to find. Dried porcini, which are readily available in food stores, are a good substitute. If you have only small amounts of the fresh mushrooms, you can fortify your dish by adding some dried porcini; it is quite good that way.

Suggested wines: Corvo Rosso or Regaleali Rosso

2 tablespoons extra virgin olive oil

3 ounces pancetta, sliced ¼ inch thick and cut into ¼-inch dice

12 ounces or more fresh porcini mushrooms, or 1 ounce dried

Sea salt to taste

Freshly ground black pepper

2 large cloves garlic, finely chopped

1 tomato, cored, peeled, and diced small

1 cup dry white wine

1½ pounds fresh pappardelle, or 1 pound dry

¼ cup coarsely chopped fresh Italian parsley

Generous pinch of crushed red pepper flakes

Put the oil into a large skillet over medium heat and add the pancetta. Sauté until golden. Set aside.

Clean the fresh porcini with a small brush or wipe with a clean kitchen towel. (Do not wash them in water, because they get water-logged easily.) If you use dried porcini, soak them for 20 minutes in warm water to cover by at least 3 inches. Wring out as much water as you can, leave them in large pieces, and strain the soaking water to remove any debris and sand. (Use the flavored water in other dishes such as sauces or as a base for soup—do not waste it.)

Add the mushrooms, salt, and pepper to the pancetta. Cook, while stirring, about 3 minutes, or until golden. Add the garlic and cook for about 1 minute. Add the tomato and white wine, stir well, and cook for about 5 minutes.

Cook the pasta al dente (see pages 28–29), and drain, leaving it wet. Be sure the sauce is hot, then add the pasta and the parsley to it, and toss well together. Serve immediately on heated plates, sprinkling on the pepper flakes.

Maccheroni con Bocconcini

(Macaroni with Small Mozzarella Balls)

SERVES 6

This dish is a genuine taste sensation. *Bocconcini* literally means "mouthfuls" or "little bites," of mozzarella cheese. In Rome, I eat them smothered in fresh heavy cream. In small portions, this dish of macaroni is elegant and tasty as a first course. As a main dish, all you have to add is a salad or a morsel or two of meat or fowl, and you have a mighty satisfying meal. The cheese will be very stringy, so it is a little challenging to eat. For a fun-loving crowd you can supply plastic scissors to cut the strings of cheese that go from plate to mouth! The flavors are fresh, and it is a dish you will make often. Suggested wines: Chianti Classico or Montepulciano d'Abruzzo

4 tablespoons extra virgin olive oil

1 pound tomatoes, cored, peeled, and chopped medium-coarse

Sea salt to taste

Freshly ground black pepper

1 pound of any short, stubby pasta such as ciufetti, penne, conchiglie, rigatoncini, or chifferi

8 ounces bocconcini, cut in half

1 cup fresh or frozen tiny peas

1 cup or more grated Parmigiano-Reggiano cheese

⅓ bunch basil, julienned

Put the oil into a large skillet over medium heat and add the tomatoes. Add the salt and pepper, and sauté until the tomatoes collapse a bit, about 4 minutes.

Cook the pasta al dente (see pages 28–29), and drain, leaving it wet.

Add the bocconcini and peas to the sauce and toss. Mix in the pasta and toss well again. Serve on very hot plates. Sprinkle on generous amounts of the Parmigiano-Reggiano, and sprinkle the basil all over the top. Eat the pasta while very hot.

Tagliatelle con Ostriche e Panna

(Tagliatelle Pasta with Oysters and Cream)

SERVES 6

Shellfish lovers really like this dish. It is very tasty, briny, and reminds one of the seashore. If you don't shuck your own oysters, I find that jarred ones from a reliable fishmonger are perfectly fine to use. This is a great dish to make late at night. It satisfies the hunger, yet it is not heavy. A big and earthy, moderately chilled white wine is a perfect accompaniment. Afterwards, I love to serve a bowl of cold oranges and a small tray of dark chocolates.

For a rich variation, use ½ cup wine and add 1 cup of heavy cream, let the sauce reduce for about 3 minutes over medium heat, and proceed as directed.

Suggested wines: Cirò Rosato or Vermentino

5 ounces unsalted butter

3 cloves garlic, finely chopped

1 cup dry white wine

Sea salt to taste

Freshly ground black pepper

1½ pounds fresh tagliatelle, spaghettini, linguine, or capellini, or 1 pound dry

4 scallions, washed, trimmed, and cut into ½-inch pieces

24 small or 18 medium shucked oysters

¼ bunch fresh spinach, well washed and trimmed

1 tablespoon or so freshly squeezed lemon juice

Put the butter into a large skillet over medium heat and add the garlic. Sauté until the garlic becomes light gold and fragrant. Add the wine, and let it reduce for about 3 minutes. Add the salt and pepper, and keep warm.

Cook the pasta al dente (see pages 28–29), and drain, leaving it slightly wet.

Meanwhile, add the scallions, oysters, spinach, and lemon juice to the sauce. Let simmer for about 2 minutes. Add the drained pasta to the sauce and toss well.

Serve immediately on heated plates. Sprinkle on plenty more pepper.

Stuffed Pasta
(Paste Ripiene)

Ravioli

(Stuffed Pasta Pillows)

SERVES 8

The fillings for ravioli are as varied as the people who make them. The word comes from the Genovese *robiole*, meaning "rubbish," or in our case, leftovers. Use your imagination and make your own ravioli dish. It is very difficult to make a "real" ravioli stuffing because it is so often determined by what is at hand. For instance, you may substitute the same quantity (and quality) of ground chicken and veal for the meats used in this recipe. All kinds of rollers, molds, and forms are available to help you shape and seal the ravioli. If you plan to make them frequently, you may find some of these utensils useful. Suggested wines: Cabernet Sauvignon or Vino Nobile di Montepulciano

2 tablespoons extra virgin olive oil

1 cup ground pork

1 cup ground beef

2 ounces Prosciutto di Parma or mortadella, finely ground

½ cup best-quality boiled ham, finely ground

1 clove garlic, minced

2 generous gratings of fresh nutmeg

½ cup freshly grated Parmesan cheese plus additional for passing

Salt and pepper

2 whole eggs

1 batch 3-egg pasta dough (see pages 18–19), covered with plastic wrap

1 quart Salsa al Pomodoro (Quick Tomato Sauce, see page 47)

To make the filling, heat the oil over medium heat, add the pork and beef, and gently cook until the meat loses its red color (unless you are already using cooked leftover meat). Set aside to cool. When the meat is cool, combine with the next 7 ingredients and blend them into a smooth paste.

Divide the pasta dough into 4 equal pieces. (You will need 2 broad sheets of pasta to make each sheet of ravioli.) Roll out one piece of pasta dough into a sheet no more than $^1\!/_{16}$ inch thick (thinner is even better). Keep the remaining 3 pieces of pasta covered while you work with the first piece. (Do not dry the pasta; for stuffed pasta, the dough must stick to itself.) Immediately begin to place the filling, 1 tablespoon at a time, in even rows across

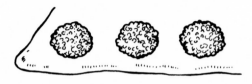

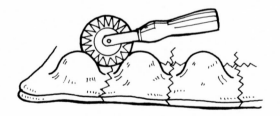

and down the sheet of pasta, about 1½ inches apart. Roll a second sheet of pasta the same size and thickness as the first. Place the second sheet on top of the first, and, with your fingers, press down between the mounds of filling to form ravioli squares. Cut out the squares, following the pressed lines with a crimped pastry cutter. If the pasta is a little dry, moisten the edges with beaten egg or water to help seal the dough. Set the ravioli aside to rest on a floured cloth. Do not pile them up, because they will stick to each other. Repeat with the remaining pasta dough. Just before serving, cook the ravioli (see pages 28–29). Drain well, and lay them in a heated dish. Pour the sauce on top and serve hot, passing the additional cheese at the table.

Note: You can freeze uncooked ravioli, tortellini, cappelleti, agnolotti, pansoti, and tortelloni. Just put them in a single layer on a baking sheet and freeze. When they are frozen, pack in jars or zip-type plastic bags for later use. When ready to cook, drop them into boiling water while they are still frozen. Add 1 minute to the cooking time.

Tortellini
(Stuffed Rings of Pasta)
MAKES ABOUT 300

These nuggets of sheer delight are loved by everyone who eats them in their many sauces and in *brodo* (broth). Mention a soup in Bologna, where these are made, and you will immediately hear about Tortellini in Brodo. To serve, allot 18 tortellini in soup per person, and about 24 in sauce per person. For freezing instructions, see the note on page 95.

To make Tortellini in Brodo for 8, cook 150 tortellini in 2½ quarts golden or brown broth (pages 114–115) until tender. Serve hot and pass grated Parmigiano-Reggiano at the table. (Heavenly!) Tortellini are also delicious in a Balsamella sauce (page 50) with a little Parmesan; with melted butter and grated cheese; or with tomato sauce and cheese. Or, they can be even tastier when baked in a preheated 400° oven for 10 to 12 minutes, or until they get a little brown at the edges.
Suggested wine: Chianti Riserva

2 tablespoons unsalted butter
4 ounces lean pork, finely ground
4 ounces veal, finely ground
2 ounces chicken breast, finely ground
1 ounce mortadella, finely ground
2 slices Prosciutto di Parma, finely ground
½ pound fresh ricotta
½ cup grated Parmesan cheese
1 egg, beaten
Scant ½ teaspoon or 1 generous grating of nutmeg
Salt and pepper to taste
1 batch 4-egg pasta dough (see pages 18–19), covered with plastic wrap

To make the filling, melt the butter in a frying pan over very low heat. Add the pork and cook for about 2 minutes. Then add the veal and chicken and cook for 7 or 8 minutes more. Set aside to cool completely, or, better yet, until cold. Add all the other ingredients except the pasta dough and broth and mix very well. Taste and adjust the seasonings; the flavors should be pronounced because you will be using tiny amounts.

Roll a piece of pasta dough into a sheet no more than $1/16$ inch thick (thinner is better). Work with one sheet at a time, cutting it immediately after rolling. This pasta should be very soft; do not dry it. With a cookie cutter or the mouth of a glass, stamp out circles of

pasta that are 2 inches in diameter. Put ½
teaspoon of filling in the center of each pasta
circle, and fold it in half like a turnover,
except that the top edge should extend
beyond the bottom edge (if the edges are
flush, the doubled layers in the rings will be
too thick). Press the top edge down firmly so
that the edges stick and will not come apart.

With the straight side of the half circle
facing you, take the two points at the ends,
wrap them around your index finger so they
overlap, and press them together to seal.
While wrapping, rotate the curved side up
toward your fingertip. If your fingers aren't
too big, you will produce a stuffed pasta ring.
(If you have very large fingers, you will have a
very large pasta ring—your tortellini would
not be admired in Bologna.) Repeat until you
have used all the pasta dough.

Cook the tortellini al dente (see pages
28–29). (Cook in broth if making soup.) Drain
well, and serve one of the ways recommended
above.

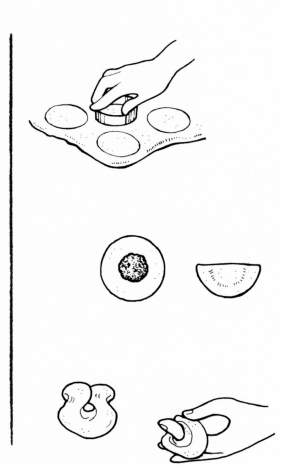

Cappelletti
(Little Hats)

MAKES ABOUT 300

Like tortellini, cappelletti can be cooked in a rich homemade chicken or veal broth and served as a first course with a spoonful of grated Parmesan; in a Balsamella sauce (page 50) with a little Parmesan; with melted butter and grated cheese; or with tomato sauce and cheese. Or, they can be baked in a preheated 400° oven for 10 to 12 minutes, or until they get a little brown at the edges. Suggested wine: Chianti Riserva

2 tablespoons unsalted butter

4 ounces lean pork, finely ground

4 ounces veal, finely ground

2 ounces chicken breast, finely ground

1 ounce mortadella, finely ground

2 slices Prosciutto di Parma, finely ground

½ pound fresh ricotta

½ cup grated Parmesan cheese

1 egg, beaten

Scant ½ teaspoon or 1 generous grating of nutmeg

Salt and pepper to taste

1 batch 4-egg pasta dough (see pages 18–19), covered with plastic wrap

To make the filling, melt the butter in a frying pan over very low heat. Add the pork and cook for about 2 minutes. Then add the veal and chicken and cook for 7 or 8 minutes more. Set aside to cool completely, or, better yet, until cold. Add all the other ingredients except the pasta dough and broth and mix very well. Taste and adjust the seasonings; the flavors should be pronounced because you will be using tiny amounts.

Roll a piece of pasta dough into a sheet no more than $\frac{1}{16}$ inch thick (thinner is better). Work with one sheet at a time, cutting it into $1\frac{1}{2}$ by $1\frac{1}{2}$-inch squares with a pastry cutter. Put $\frac{1}{4}$ teaspoon of filling in the center of each pasta square. Fold the squares into small triangles with the top part extending beyond the bottom part. With the long side of a filled triangle facing you, wrap the triangle around your finger and press the ends together to seal, leaving the top of the triangle sticking up to resemble a bishop's miter. Repeat until all the pasta dough is used.

Cook the cappelletti al dente (see pages 28–29). Drain well, and serve one of the ways recommended above. (Cook in broth if making soup.)

Agnolotti

(Round Stuffed Pasta "Lambs")

SERVES 6

Agnolotti ("little lambs"), in case you haven't guessed, are ravioli in sheep's clothing. So many Italian names are whimsical and express someone's imagination, adding to the maddening confusion of trying to identify and codify Italian dishes. Thank heaven they are so delicious! An error in name will still get you a gastronomic treat. For freezing instructions, see the note on page 95.

Suggested wines: Valpolicella or Corvo Rosso

2 bunches spinach, well washed

8 tablespoons unsalted butter

1 small yellow onion, finely diced

½ pound ground beef

1 slice mortadella, finely chopped

½ cup freshly grated Parmesan cheese

Salt and pepper to taste

1 batch 3-egg pasta dough (see pages 18-19), covered with plastic wrap

1 quart Salsa di Pomodoro Stracotto (Slow Tomato Sauce, see page 46)

Shake the excess water from the spinach and steam it in a covered pot, using only the water left on the leaves. When it has just "collapsed," remove the lid and let it dry out a bit over low heat. Set it aside to cool.

Melt the butter in a frying pan over medium-low heat. Add the onion and cook just until it is transparent. Add the beef and cook just until it loses its red color. Set aside to cool.

Combine the mortadella, ¼ cup of the Parmesan, and the salt and pepper. Combine the mixture with the cooled spinach and beef; blend well.

Divide the pasta dough into 4 equal pieces and roll and fill as instructed for making ravioli (see page 94). With your fingers, press down all around the mounds of filling in a circular shape. Cut out the agnlotti by placing the mouth of a shot glass, a cookie cutter, or an agnolotti cutter over the circular seal and pressing. If the pasta is a little dry, moisten the edges with beaten egg or water to help seal the dough. Set the agnolotti aside to rest on a floured cloth. Do not pile them up because they will stick to each other. Repeat with the remaining pasta dough.

Just before serving, cook the agnolotti al dente (see pages 28–29). Meanwhile, heat the sauce. Drain the agnolotti, transfer to a heated dish, cover with sauce, and serve. Pass the remaining ¼ cup of cheese at the table.

Conchiglie Ripieni
(Stuffed Pasta Shells)
SERVES 6 TO 8

This is an excellent dish for entertaining as it can be assembled in advance, frozen, and cooked or reheated just before serving. Two or 3 make a perfect first course; 5 or 6 make a main dish. A nice variation is to make two fillings, one with meat and the other with ricotta and spinach. There are about 40 pasta shells in a pound. Some may break—use them in soup. You can easily cut this recipe in half. Or freeze extras in an ovenproof dish, then bake covered (and unthawed) at 350° for 1½ hours. Suggested wines: Cabernet Sauvignon or Chianti Riserva

1 quart Balsamella (White Sauce, see page 50)
2 pounds ricotta
¼ pound Prosciutto di Parma, finely minced
1 cup mozzarella, finely diced
¼ cup finely chopped fresh Italian parsley
2 eggs
Salt and pepper to taste
1 pound jumbo dried pasta shells
1 pint Salsa al Pomodoro (Quick Tomato Sauce, see page 47)
½ cup grated Parmesan or Romano cheese

Prepare two 9 by 14-inch ovenproof casserole dishes or one large roasting pan by spreading a ⅛-inch layer of Balsamella on the bottom; set aside.

Mix the ricotta, prosciutto, mozzarella, parsley, and eggs together in a bowl. Adjust salt and pepper. Set aside.

Cook the pasta shells *very* al dente (about 1½ minutes less than the package directs.) Drain the shells and plunge them into cold water to stop the cooking process. Drain again and place them on an oiled tray.

Fill the shells with the ricotta mixture, using a pastry tube. A spoon or knife will work, but that method is very slow. Place the filled shells on the bed of white sauce, arranging them fairly close together.

Put some more white sauce on top of the shells, and then drizzle Salsa al Pomodoro over that. Sprinkle the Parmesan on top.

Preheat the oven to 350°. Bake the conchiglie for about 30 to 40 minutes. Serve very hot.

Note: You can totally assemble this dish and freeze it. However, it should not be thawed before heating, because the pasta will become soggy. Freeze it in an ovenproof dish and simply bake it covered (and frozen) in a 350° oven for about 1½ hours before serving.

Pansoti con Salsa di Noci

(Pasta Pillows of Ricotta with Walnut Sauce)

SERVES 8

I would serve this dish with broiled or roasted meat or fowl. For freezing instructions, see the note on page 95.

Suggested wines: A bold red wine such as Aglianico or Gattinara

1 pound Swiss chard

1 bunch watercress (or borage)

2 whole eggs

⅔ cup ricotta

**½ cup grated Parmigiano-Reggiano
   cheese**

2 generous gratings of fresh nutmeg

Salt and pepper to taste

**1 batch 4-egg pasta dough (see pages
   18-19), covered with plastic wrap**

½ pound walnut meats

3 tablespoons pine nuts

1 small clove garlic

3 tablespoons fresh Italian parsley

**⅓ cup curdled milk (add a few drops
   of lemon juice to warmed milk and
   let it stand at room temperature
   for 15 to 30 minutes)**

½ cup extra virgin olive oil

**Grated Parmigiano-Reggiano cheese
   for passing**

To make the filling, wash the chard well in cold water. Shake out the excess water and steam the chard in a covered pan just until done—it should not be mushy. Drain well. Put the chard in a food processor, or chop finely by hand. Add the watercress, eggs, ricotta, Parmigiano-Reggiano, nutmeg, and salt and pepper. Blend well. If the mixture looks too wet or runny, add a little more grated Parmesan, or 1 tablespoon of bread crumbs. Set aside.

Divide the pasta dough into 4 equal pieces and roll and fill as instructed for making ravioli (see page 94). With your fingers, press down around the mounds of filling to form triangles. Cut out the pansoti with a crimped pastry wheel. If the pasta is a little dry, moisten the edges with beaten egg or water to help seal the dough. Set the pansoti aside to rest on a floured cloth. Do not pile them up, because they will stick to each other. Repeat with the remaining pasta dough.

Put the walnuts, pine nuts, garlic, and parsley into the food processor and blend them into a smooth paste. Add the curdled milk and mix well; then add the oil and blend some more.

Cook the pansoti al dente (see pages 28-29). Drain well, and lay them in a heated dish. Add the sauce and toss well. Serve hot, passing the Parmigiano-Reggiano at the table.

Cannelloni

(Stuffed Large Reeds)

SERVES 6

Everyone loves cannelloni. Small ones can be a delicious first course in a large meal and large ones make a whole meal when served with a salad.

Suggested wines: Verdicchio or Pinot Bianco

**1 bunch spinach, or 10 ounces
    frozen**

**1 yellow onion peeled, finely
    chopped**

2 tablespoons olive oil

¼ pound ground beef or veal

**½ cup finely chopped mortadella or
    unsmoked ham**

2 generous gratings of fresh nutmeg

**¼ cup freshly grated Parmesan
    cheese plus additional for passing**

1 egg, beaten

**1 batch 3-egg pasta dough (see
    pages 18–19), covered with
    plastic wrap**

**2 quarts Salsa al Pomodoro (Quick
    Tomato Sauce, see page 47)**

**1 pint Balsamella (White Sauce, see
    page 50)**

Cook the spinach just until it begins to collapse. Drain it well and chop medium-fine. Set aside.

Put the onion, oil, beef, and mortadella in a frying pan and cook until all are done. Add the spinach, nutmeg, and cheese. Mix thoroughly and set aside to cool. Stir in the egg.

Roll the pasta out in large sheets less than ¹⁄₁₆ inch thick. Cut the sheets into rectangles about 4 by 5 inches (to yield 12 pieces).

Bring a stockpot of water to a boil, and add some salt. Drop in 2 or 3 pieces of pasta at a time and cook for about 1 minute. Lift them out and plunge into cold water to stop the cooking. Lay them on damp towels to keep moist.

Spread a generous row of filling down the long side of each rectangle and roll them up, starting with the long side. Place the filled cannelloni in a well-buttered ovenproof baking dish. Spread evenly with one or both sauces. Sprinkle the additional cheese over the top and bake in a 375° oven for about 20 minutes.

Note: You can prepare the cannelloni up to 1 day ahead. Store covered in the refrigerator. Let the cannelloni come to room temperature before baking as directed. As a variation, you can substitute 1 pound of ricotta cheese for the meats.

Tortelloni
(Tortelloni as Made in Tuscany)

SERVES 4 TO 6

This is an unusual and delicious stuffed pasta, which should only be made fresh. For freezing instructions, see the note on page 95.

Suggested wines: Barbera or Chianti Riserva

**8 ounces finely ground pork meat
    with some fat**

3 to 4 tablespoons dry white wine

Salt and pepper to taste

1 large clove garlic, minced

**3 to 4 tablespoons minced fresh
    Italian parsley**

1 to 2 tablespoons tomato paste

¼ cup grated Parmesan cheese

3 to 4 tablespoons bread crumbs

2 eggs

**Generous pinch of crushed red
    pepper flakes**

**1 batch 3-egg pasta dough (see
    pages 18–19), covered with
    plastic wrap**

16 tablespoons unsalted butter

8 to 10 fresh sage leaves, torn in thirds

1 cup grated Parmesan cheese

Freshly ground black pepper

To make the filling, cook the pork until just done. Add the wine and cook for about 2 minutes more. Set aside to cool, and when cool, add the next 7 ingredients and mix well.

Divide the pasta dough into 4 equal pieces and roll and fill as instructed for making ravioli (see page 94), except roll sheets no more than ⅛ inch thick and place filling 2½ inches apart. With your fingers, press down between the mounds of filling to form large squares, about 2½ by 2½ inches. Cut out the squares, following the pressed lines with a crimped pastry cutter. If the pasta is a little dry, moisten the edges with beaten egg or water to help seal the dough. Set the tortelloni aside to rest on a floured cloth. Do not pile them up, because they will stick to each other. Repeat with the remaining pasta dough.

Cook the tortelloni al dente (see pages 28–29).

While the tortelloni cook, make the sauce. Melt the butter over *very* low heat; do not cook. When melted, add the sage leaves and stir well. Keep hot.

Drain the tortelloni. Put a little of the sauce on the bottom of a heated serving dish. Add a layer of tortelloni, then sauce, and then grated cheese, and repeat until you end up with butter sauce and cheese on top. Top with the pepper and serve hot.

Baked Pasta
(Pasta al Forno)

Lasagne
(Baked Filled Pasta Sheets)
SERVES 8 OR 10

This could very well be the single most popular pasta dish known outside of Italy. I love to eat it, and I am always delighted to be served lasagne when invited out to dinner.

If you like, use spinach pasta (see pages 22–23) for a change.

Instead of cutting the pasta into wide noodles, you can cut it the very old-fashioned way, using the crimped cutter to make squarish pieces about 3 by 3 inches or 3 by 4 inches. These pieces were thrown into the layered casserole at random in the way you would deal a deck of cards—still a nice effect today.

Suggested wines: My choice would be a good red wine like a Cabernet Sauvignon or a Chianti. However, there is nothing wrong with an equally stout white wine like a Chardonnay or an Orvieto.

2½ quarts Salsa di Pomodoro
  Stracotto (Slow Tomato Sauce, see
  page 46 and instructions below)
¾ pound ground beef
¼ pound ground pork
1 cup fresh or frozen tiny peas
1 batch 3-egg plain or spinach pasta
  dough (see pages 18–19, 22–23),
  covered with plastic wrap
1 pound ricotta (optional)
1 cup grated Parmesan cheese
1 cup shredded mozzarella cheese

Prepare the sauce as directed, adding the ground meats with the onion and garlic. Cook until the meats have lost their red color before you proceed with the rest of the sauce. Add the peas to the sauce, just before you remove it from the heat.

Butter a rectangular 9 by 14-inch baking dish and set it aside.

Roll out the dough into large pasta sheets and dry them as directed (see pages 20–21). Then cut them into traditional lasagne strips about 12 inches long and 1½ to 2 inches wide. Or, to save some work, you can cut the sheets the same size as your baking dish. Use a crimped pastry cutter if you want a fancier edge.

Cook the pasta *very* al dente (see pages 28–29), a few at a time. Remove them with a slotted spoon and plunge them into cold water to stop cooking. Lay them on a damp towel.

Preheat the oven to 375°.

Layer first the pasta and then the sauce alternately in the prepared casserole. Incorporate a layer or two of ricotta, between the layers of pasta and sauce. Sprinkle the Parmesan and mozzarella on the top and dot with a bit more sauce. Bake 25 to 40 minutes. Serve piping hot.

Sformato di Pasta

(Pasta "Soufflé")

SERVES 10

A *sformato*, which simply means molded, is different from a soufflé in that it is usually turned out of its mold and onto its plate. You can do that with this dish if you like. It does not rise as much as a typical soufflé. It makes a luscious and delicate first course, even more elegant in individual ovenproof ramekins. I believe this must be a relatively new recipe because I can't imagine the old-time Italians going to such pains with a perfectly good dish of pasta. Your guests are bound to enjoy this.

Suggested wines: A light wine like Vermentino would be a good choice, or you might try a Frascati.

1 tablespoon unsalted butter

1 small shallot, finely chopped

½ pound boiled ham, finely chopped

¾ cup grated Parmigiano-Reggiano cheese

Salt and pepper to taste

Generous grating of fresh nutmeg

1 batch 2-egg plain or spinach pasta dough (see pages 18–19, 22–23), cut as fettuccine

5 whole eggs, separated

1 cup Balsamella (White Sauce, see page 50)

Melt the butter in a heavy pan over low heat, add the shallot, and cook until it is transparent.

Add the ham and stir. Add the cheese, salt, pepper, and nutmeg and stir again. Let the mixture cool completely.

Cook the fettuccine al dente (see pages 28–29), drain well, and let cool. Add the ham mixture, the egg yolks, and the Balsamella to the pasta. Mix together thoroughly.

Butter a 3 to 3½-quart soufflé dish generously. Preheat the oven to 375°.

Beat the egg whites until they are stiff and shiny. Fold them carefully into the pasta mixture and pour it into the soufflé dish. Bake in the middle of the oven for about 40 minutes, or until the soufflé has risen and turned a lovely light brown. Serve immediately.

Pasta al Forno
(Baked Macaroni)

SERVES 8 TO 12

This is a famous and traditional dish in Italy, particularly in and around Palermo in Sicily. It is a dish used for festive occasions when families gather, Christmas being one of the most important. It is a wonderful dish for a very large party, especially a buffet, because it is plentiful and easy to serve. To me this dish is much like the wonderful madeleines were to Marcel Proust in his memoirs. Boyhood memories leap forth when I eat Pasta al Forno, which was always made with such love by my family. Suggested wines: Chianti Classico would be a good choice. The wonderful Corvo Rosso is perfect with this dish. Whichever red wine you choose should have some age and be quite robust.

2½ quarts plus a little extra Salsa di Pomodoro Stracotto (Slow Tomato Sauce, see page 47 and instructions below)

2 pounds beef rump or pork butt roast

½ cup bread crumbs

4 hard-boiled eggs

1½ pounds best-quality commercial large or small dried pasta, such as spaghetti, rotelle, mostaccioli, or rigatoni

1 cup fresh or frozen tiny peas

¾ cup grated Romano or Parmesan cheese

Salt to taste

Freshly ground black pepper to taste

Prepare the sauce as directed, including the meat in one solid piece. Cook slowly for up to 3 hours.

Prepare a 4-quart ovenproof casserole by spreading a moderate amount of shortening on its sides and bottom. Pour in ¼ cup of the bread crumbs and twist and turn the casserole until the sides and bottom are evenly coated. Gently shake out any excess. Set aside.

Remove the piece of meat from the sauce and let it cool to room temperature. Shred it with a fork. (Do not cut it if possible.) Set aside.

Slice the hard-boiled eggs about ¼ inch thick, and set aside.

Cook the pasta *very* al dente (see pages 28–29), and drain well. Return the pasta to the cooking pot and toss it in a very small amount of the tomato sauce.

Assemble the casserole, starting with a generous layer of pasta, a generous layer of shredded meat, some egg slices, some peas, some grated cheese, some sauce, and sprinkle on a little salt and pepper. Repeat, finishing with a layer of pasta. Sprinkle the top with cheese, the remaining ¼ cup bread crumbs, and a little more sauce.

Bake in a preheated 350° oven for about 1½ hours. When the top and sides are golden brown, remove from the oven and let it rest 20 minutes before serving. It may also be turned out on a plate or a cutting board and sliced as you would a cake. Extra sauce may be served with the slices, though it is neither necessary nor traditional.

Note: Any leftover sauce will store well in the refrigerator for up to 5 days; it can also be frozen for some time.

Penne in Cestino di Melanzane

(Penne Pasta in an Eggplant Basket)

SERVES 6

This pretty dish may seem fussy, but it actually has big, earthy flavors and can be prepared in advance. Suggested wines: Merlot from Fruili-Venezia Giulia or Rosso del Salento

About ½ cup extra virgin olive oil

1 large eggplant with skin on, washed and cut crosswise into 12 ¾-inch-thick slices

2 cloves garlic, finely chopped

2 pounds juicy, ripe tomatoes, peeled, cored, and finely chopped

Sea salt to taste

Freshly ground black pepper to taste

1 pound penne pasta

¾ pound fresh mozzarella, cut into tiny dice

½ cup fresh or frozen tiny peas

1 big bunch fresh basil

1½ cups grated Parmigiano-Reggiano cheese

Heat all but 1 tablespoon of the oil in a frying pan and fry the eggplant slices until they are deep gold and tender. Set aside. To conserve oil, brush the slices with oil and broil them. Turn once during cooking. You can do this the day before and reheat the eggplant in the oven.

Sauté the garlic in the remaining 1 tablespoon of oil. Add the tomatoes and cook for about 10 to 12 minutes. If the mixture looks a little dry, add some hot water or red wine. The sauce should be medium-thick. Add the salt and pepper.

Line 6 ovenproof custard cups or bowls of 2-cup capacity with 2 overlapping slices of eggplant.

Cook the pasta al dente (see pages 28–29), and drain, leaving it slightly wet. Return the pasta to the cooking pot. Add the hot tomato sauce, cheese, and peas. (If the peas are small enough, the heat will cook them. If not, pre-cook them for about 3 minutes in lightly salted water. Drain and use as directed.)

Chop the basil and mix it into the pasta. Divide the pasta evenly among the bowls, placing it on top of the eggplant slices. (It is alright to dome it up a bit in the middle.) Sprinkle 2 teaspoons of the cheese on each portion.

Bake in a preheated 400° oven for about 12 to 15 minutes. If the pasta seems to be drying, cover it loosely with light-weight foil.

Place a warm dinner plate over each bowl and carefully turn it over so that the eggplant-draped pasta pops out onto the plate. Serve piping hot, passing the remaining cheese at the table.

Vermicelli al Forno
(Ultrathin Pasta, Baked)
SERVES 6

My own family have grown very fond of this dish served as a delicate first-course pasta. We do it *sformato*, turned out of individual ovenproof ramekins onto a light tomato sauce covering the center of a small plate. It makes a decorative and tasty starter for an important meal. With the distinctive taste of the slightly bitter black olives, it is particularly good before an entrée with a strong flavor, such as roasted or braised fowl or game.

Suggested wines: Chardonnay or Pinot Grigio

8 black Sicilian or calamata olives, pitted and coarsely chopped

4 slices of Prosciutto di Parma, finely chopped

A few large capers, chopped

3 to 4 tablespoons bread crumbs

⅔ cup chopped fresh Italian parsley

4 teaspoons Extra virgin olive oil

Salt and pepper to taste

12 ounces vermicelli

2 whole eggs, beaten

⅓ cup grated Parmigiano-Reggiano cheese

1 cup Salsa al Pomodoro (Quick Tomato Sauce, see page 47), plus 1 or 2 spoonfuls of heavy cream (optional)

Generously butter a small ovenproof casserole, or individual ovenproof dishes that will just hold all the ingredients. Set aside.

Preheat the oven to 400°. Make the "sauce" by putting the olives, prosciutto, capers, bread crumbs, parsley, the oil, and salt and pepper into a frying pan to cook gently. Heat everything just through to blend the flavors. Set aside.

Meanwhile, cook the pasta al dente (see pages 28–29). (Be careful because this pasta is thin and cooks very quickly.) Drain the pasta well, return it to the cooking pot, and toss it in a little oil to keep it from sticking together. Add the "sauce" and mix thoroughly. Put the mixture into the prepared casserole or individual dishes. Pour the beaten eggs over the pasta and sprinkle on the cheese.

Bake about 15 minutes, or until a lovely golden crust is formed on the top and, with luck, also on the sides. Remove from the oven and allow to rest for a few minutes. Combine the Salsa al Pomodoro and cream, spoon the mixture onto a serving platter, and turn out the pasta onto the sauce. If the pasta is well set, you could turn it out onto a plate and cut into wedges as you would cut a pie.

Pasta in Broths and Soups
(Pasta in Brodo e Minestre)

Brodo di Carne
(Meat Broth)
MAKES 2 GENEROUS QUARTS

The terms "broth" and "stock" are interchangeable these days. For our purposes we will stick with broth, because it sounds comforting. You can make broth with only vegetables and water, but here we will use meat. When broth is made well, it is satisfying, and sipping a bowl of it gives a sense of well-being. Many home cooks feel you can't run a kitchen without it.

Basic broths, golden and brown ones, are easy to make and can be used as the base for soups and sauces in many dishes. Most golden broths are made with chicken or veal meat (turkey wings work well, too). The following recipe can easily be cut in half. This broth will keep covered in the refrigerator for 3 days. It freezes well for up to 3 months if tightly sealed in a plastic or glass container. Strained broth can be intensified by boiling it over medium-high heat without a lid for 45 minutes more after it is cooled and strained. Skim off any scum that may rise to the surface.

2 yellow onions, cut into quarters

2 carrots, cut into 1-inch pieces

2 stalks celery, cut into 1-inch pieces

10 black peppercorns

3 cloves garlic

2 bay leaves, torn in half

¼ teaspoon dry oregano

3 pounds chicken backs, necks, and bones, or 1 whole chicken cut into 12 or more pieces

Salt to taste

3 quarts cold water

Place all the ingredients in a 6-quart stockpot. Put the pot over medium heat until it just begins to simmer. Reduce the heat to low, and simmer for about 4 hours, skimming occasionally. Do not stir. If you use a whole chicken, remove after 1½ hours of cooking, and let the broth simmer for the remaining 1½ hours. (Use the meat as you wish.)

When the broth has finished cooking, let it cool undisturbed. Carefully strain it into a clean saucepan, using a fine-holed colander. Discard the bones and vegetables. Lightly salt the broth before using.

Brodo di Carne Scuro
(Dark Meat Broth)

Brown, or dark, broth is made the same way as golden, except that the bones are roasted before they go in the stockpot. The storage and reduction instructions are the same for this broth as for the Brodo di Carne (opposite page).

4 pounds veal bones, cracked and cut into 2- to 3-inch pieces
2 yellow onions, cut into quarters
2 carrots, cut into 1-inch pieces
2 stalks celery, cut into 1-inch pieces
3 cloves garlic
2 tablespoons tomato paste
10 black peppercorns
3 quarts of cold water
2 bay leaves, torn in half
Salt to taste

Preheat the oven to 400°.

Place the bones and vegetables in a single layer in a large roasting pan. Roast for about 30 minutes, turning them every 10 minutes or so. Smear the tomato paste on the bones, and return to the oven for 20 more minutes, or until the bones and vegetables are dark brown. Put the contents of the roasting pan in a 6-quart stockpot, add the peppercorns, bay leaves, and water.

Put the pot over medium heat until it just begins to simmer. Reduce the heat to low, and simmer for about 4 hours, skimming occasionally. Do not stir. When the broth has finished cooking, let it cool undisturbed. Carefully strain it into a clean saucepan, using a fine-holed colander. Discard the bones and vegetables. Lightly salt the broth before using.

Tagliatelle Rosa

(Fresh Pasta with Boiled Beef Tongue)

SERVES 6

This minestra, characteristically Italian, certainly makes a full meal when followed by a salad and fruit, and it is a very nice way to enjoy a specialty meat. You may substitute 4 ounces shredded prosciutto for half the quantity of tongue, or use only 4 ounces of shredded prosciutto. For this recipe, you will have to decide whether to cook your pasta in the broth or separately in plain water. If you have an abundance of good stock, you may want the added flavor of pasta cooked in stock, especially if it is fresh pasta and will cook quickly. Be forewarned that the pasta will absorb some of the liquid and reduce the volume of stock. If, on the other hand, you are short of stock or broth, and especially if you are using commercial dried pasta instead of the fresh, it is probably best to cook the pasta separately in plain water.

1 tablespoon extra virgin olive oil

A little pork fat (size of a walnut)

1 yellow onion, finely chopped

8 ounces boiled fresh beef tongue, julienned

1½ to 2 quarts chicken or veal broth

1 batch fresh 3-egg pasta dough (see pages 18–19), cut into ribbons and covered in plastic wrap

Salt and pepper to taste

Put the olive oil, fat, and onion into a frying pan over medium heat and gently cook until the onion is soft and translucent. Add the tongue and cook for a couple of minutes more.

Bring the broth to a boil and add the cooked onion and tongue. Then either add and cook the pasta in the stock, or cook it separately (see pages 28–29), drain well, and add it to the broth. Add salt and pepper. Pour the soup into a warm tureen and serve hot as a first course or as the main dish of a light meal.

Pastina in Brodo

(Little Pasta Cuts in Broth)

SERVES 6

This soup is sometimes called Zuppa Maritata. I guess the pasta is "married" to the broth, but in any case, this is a rich and satisfying way to start a meal. This soup is so simple that it demands a really good broth.

If you make your own chicken broth, there is nothing you could possibly do to improve it more than adding some chicken feet, if you can find them. The feet give a really rich, fresh chicken taste to the stock, and it's too bad that they are removed from most chickens sold to American consumers. My parents always kept their own chickens, and as a child it was my job to cut the entrails with scissors and clean them so that even the guts could go into the stockpot. I often wondered why, but today when I recall my mother's beautiful velvety chicken broth, I am sure she knew a great deal that the world has since forgotten.

If you cannot make your own chicken stock, you can still make a quart of canned chicken broth much tastier by adding a celery branch cut into medium-sized pieces, a medium-sized onion cut into 6 pieces (skin and all), 3 or 4 whole black peppercorns, and a small bay leaf. Simmer the broth for about 40 minutes, or until reduced by one-fifth, and strain through a fine sieve or wet cheesecloth. Once you get used to these good flavors, you'll find they are worth any amount of extra trouble. You can also use veal or beef broth in this recipe with delicious results.

Once again, you must decide if you have enough broth to cook the pastina in, or whether you need to conserve the broth by cooking the pasta separately in plain water and adding it already cooked. In the case of this particular soup, I believe you will get a better result if you have plenty of stock and cook the pasta in it.

1½ quarts strong chicken broth, well seasoned but clear
¾ cup pastina
2 tablespoons grated Parmigiano-Reggiano cheese

Bring the broth to a simmer.

Add the pastina and stir well. Let it simmer for about 6 or 7 minutes.

Serve the soup hot with about a teaspoonful of the cheese sprinkled on top of each portion.

Minestrone alla Genovese

(Soup Genoa-Style)

SERVES 10 OR MORE

It is very sad that the "minestrone" served in a lot of restaurants in America is heavy, mushy, water-logged, and tastes as though it has been reheated for days on end. Until you have sampled a freshly made Minestrone alla Genovese with each vegetable crisply and separately defined, you won't know what a minestrone actually is and can be. Note that this is practically a vegetarian dish, which is characteristic of the way you would find it in Italy, where an abundance of fresh in-season vegetables is as common as meat is scarce. Remember to soak the beans the night before.

If the soup then becomes too thick, add just enough boiling water or broth to thin it. Minestrone at its best is a stick-to-the-ribs soup that could easily be the mainstay of a delicious meal if you added some crusty bread, a simple green salad, and some fresh fruit and cheese.

Suggested wine: A white wine such as a Sauvignon Bianco would be very good with this dish.

2 cups dry white beans, soaked overnight in cold water
1 cup finely chopped carrots
1 cup finely chopped onions
2 cups peeled and finely chopped raw potatoes
2 cups finely chopped spinach or Swiss chard
3 quarts water
Salt to taste
½ teaspoon finely ground black pepper
½ pound small macaroni
½ cup finely chopped fresh Italian parsley
3 leaves fresh basil, finely chopped
3 ounces Prosciutto di Parma fat, pancetta fat, or bacon fat, blanched (to remove the smoky flavor), and finely chopped
2 cloves garlic, well crushed
½ cup grated Parmigiano-Reggiano cheese

Drain the beans, then put them and the next 7 ingredients into a pot and bring to a simmer. Cook gently until well blended and the beans are al dente. Add the pasta and cook until it is just al dente.

When ready to serve the minestrone, mash together the parsley, basil, fat, and garlic in a food processor or blender, or with a mortar and pestle. When it has become a nice thick mass, add it to the minestrone and stir well. Serve the minestrone piping hot and pass the cheese at the table.

Pasta e Fagioli
(Pasta and Beans)
SERVES 8

This dish is famous as *Pasta Fazool*, and can be made in many ways. Some regional variations of the basic recipe are given below (see the note). Again, this is practically a vegetarian dish and a hearty one, particularly suited to cold weather. Followed by some fresh fruit and cheese, it makes a good meal that is also good for you. Be sure to set the beans to soak the night before you plan to make this soup.

2 cups dried white cannellini or great northern beans, soaked overnight in cold water

1 ounce Prosciutto di Parma, including skin, or lean salt pork

1 large yellow onion, cut into medium dice

2 garlic cloves, peeled and well mashed

¼ cup olive oil

Salt to taste

¼ teaspoon freshly ground black pepper

½ pound small short macaroni

¼ cup grated Parmesan cheese

Drain the beans, then place them and the next 6 ingredients in a small stockpot. Add water to cover. Bring to a simmer and cook gently until the beans are soft but not mushy.

If all of the water is absorbed, add more boiling water or some stock. Add the pasta and cook until it is just done, not mushy. (Remember that the pasta will absorb some of the liquid, unless you cook it separately in plain water.) The soup should be quite dense.

Serve it hot and pass the cheese as well as the pepper mill at the table.

Note: For a Tuscan version of this soup, add a generous cup of coarsely chopped fresh or canned tomatoes. For a Venetian version, use red kidney beans instead of the white, and add a healthy pinch of cinnamon.

Fried Pasta
(Pasta Fritta)

Panzarotti
(Fried Ravioli)
SERVES 6

These tasty little morsels can be filled with other things you might have on hand, such as chopped meat or vegetables. They are delicious just as a snack, or as an appetizer with drinks before dinner. They also make an unusual first course. You can cut and fill these in squares as ravioli (see pages 94–95), or in rounds as agnolotti (see page 99). For this recipe I prefer folded rounds, also called ravioli in some parts of Italy. Use your imagination both in serving and filling them. My own favorite is a filling of ricotta, which is delicious in any form.
Suggested wines: Cannonau or Chianti

1 pound ricotta

3 ounces Prosciutto di Parma, finely chopped

¼ cup finely chopped fresh Italian parsley

Salt and pepper to taste

1 whole egg

1 batch 3-egg pasta dough (see pages 18–19), covered with plastic wrap

Olive oil for frying

Mix together the cheese, prosciutto, parsley, salt and pepper, and egg. Set the mixture aside.

Roll out the pasta into large, thin sheets. Do not let them dry out.

Cut the pasta sheet into rounds 2½ inches in diameter, using a cookie cutter or the mouth of a glass. Put a generous teaspoon of the filling on top of each one. Fold the dough over to look like a turnover and pinch the edges together to make a tight seal, using a wash of water or beaten egg to make it stick, if necessary.

Fry the panzarotti in very hot oil until golden and crisp.

Serve immediately.

Frittata di Spaghetti

(Spaghetti Omelette)

SERVES 4

This is another good way to use leftover pasta. It is a great brunch dish and makes a very nice first course. It is probably at its very best as a midnight snack. You can add other ingredients, too, such as anchovies, capers, or tuna fish to suit your taste.

Suggested wines: Cabernet Sauvignon or Montepulciano d'Abruzzo

3 tablespoons extra virgin olive oil

12 ounces cold cooked pasta, such as spaghetti, vermicelli, or linguine

3 eggs

½ cup grated Parmesan cheese

Salt and pepper to taste

¼ cup finely chopped fresh Italian parsley

¼ cup finely chopped Gaeta or calamata black olives

Put the oil in a wide, heavy nonstick frying pan over medium heat.

When it is very hot (but long before it starts to smoke), add the pasta. Spread it in the pan in a nice round, flat shape about 1½ inches high, and slightly lower the heat.

Let the pasta cook slowly for about 5 or 6 minutes, or until it is golden on the bottom. (Don't let it burn.)

Beat the eggs and add to them the cheese, salt, pepper, parsley, and olives. Pour this mixture over the pasta in the pan and gently poke it into the mass of pasta with a fork. Lower the heat.

As soon as the eggs have set, put a plate face down on top of the omelette. Invert the pan to transfer the omelette to the plate. Then gently slide the omelette off the plate and back into the frying pan and let it brown on the other side. You can eliminate this tricky maneuver by placing the frying pan of pasta under a preheated broiler until the top browns. If you do this, however, watch it carefully so that it does not burn or dry out.

When the pasta omelette is done, turn it out of the pan onto a board or serving platter. Let it rest for about 5 minutes. Cut it into wedges and serve hot, or tepid, as is done in Italy.

Crocchetti di Spaghetti

(Pasta Croquettes)

SERVES 10

This is a very attractive and delicious way to use up leftover pasta. These croquettes can be excellent with roast beef, chicken, or broiled lamp chops. You may have leftover flour, egg, and bread crumbs— I prefer to work with a generous amount.

Suggested wines: Gattinara or Barbaresco

Olive oil for frying

1 pound leftover cooked pasta, such as spaghetti, tagliatelle, or just about anything

4 to 5 ounces leftover meat, shredded

1 cup thick Balsamella (Béchamel or White Sauce, see page 50)

⅓ cup grated Parmigiano-Reggiano cheese

⅓ cup Salsa di Pomodoro Stracotto or Salsa al Pomodoro (Slow Tomato Sauce, page 46, or Quick Tomato Sauce, page 47)

Salt and pepper to taste

3 cups all-purpose flour for dredging

4 large eggs, beaten, for dipping

3 to 4 cups fine bread crumbs for dredging

Grease a shallow baking pan that has sides at least 1½ inches high with oil. Set aside.

In a saucepan, combine the pasta, meat, Balsamella, cheese, tomato sauce, salt, and pepper. Heat the mixture through and stir until it is well amalgamated.

Pour the mixture into the baking pan and spread it evenly with a spatula. It should be about 1¼ inches high. Let it cool thoroughly, in the refrigerator if necessary, until it is solidly set.

Cut it into shapes with a knife or cookie cutter. Regular bars will also do very well. Dredge the cutouts in flour, then in beaten egg, and then in bread crumbs, pressing to make sure the surface is thoroughly coated.

Line a baking pan with paper towels. Pour oil ½ inch deep into a frying pan and heat to almost smoking hot. Carefully add the croquettes and cook until golden brown. Watch carefully to make sure they don't burn, and turn them at least once to brown on as many sides as possible.

Transfer the browned croquettes to the pan lined with paper towels and place in a warm oven. You can keep them hot in the oven if you are planning to serve them right away. Or you can reheat them in a preheated 325° oven for about 10 minutes before serving. Leave the door of the oven slightly ajar so that they don't steam and become soggy.

Pasta Fritta
(Fried Pasta)
SERVES 4 TO 6

This dish makes an unusual and distinctive first course. It could be followed by roast veal with pan juices, green beans or broccoli, some cheese, and a bowl of fruit. It can also be a very friendly and warming dish to eat late at night. After a movie or an opera, when you get a case of the munchies but want something with a bit of style that's more substantial, this dish can do a good job of filling the bill. I have even eaten pasta fritta for breakfast when I couldn't face cereal or bacon and eggs. Suggested wines: My choice with this dish, served at any hour (except perhaps breakfast), is a nice Aglianico or Corvo Rosso.

⅓ cup or a little more extra virgin olive oil
8 to 9 anchovy fillets, finely chopped
12 ounces cooked long ribbon pasta or capelli d'angelo
⅓ cup grated Romano cheese
Freshly ground black pepper
Pinch of crushed red pepper flakes
4 tablespoons chopped fresh Italian parsley

Heat half of the oil in a nonstick frying pan over medium heat and add the anchovies. Cook for about 3 minutes, stirring all the time. Place the cooked pasta in a bowl. Add the anchovies and oil to the pasta and mix well. Add the cheese, black pepper, and pepper flakes to the pasta mixture and toss thoroughly.

Put the rest of the olive oil in the frying pan. When it is fairly hot, add the pasta mixture and spread it into a round shape about 1½ inches high. Fry it gently until the bottom is set and golden brown.

Put a plate on top of the pasta, face down. Carefully invert the pan, transferring the pasta to the plate. Then slide the pasta off the plate and back into the frying pan; gently fry it until the other side is golden.

Transfer the fried pasta from the pan to a heated plate. Sprinkle on the parsley, cut the pasta into wedges, and serve hot.

[INDEX]

Select Sources for Italian Ingredients and Kitchenwares

Balducci's
424 6th Avenue
New York, NY 10011
(212) 673-2600
(212) 915-5065 (fax)

Vivande Porta Via
2125 Fillmore Street
San Francisco, CA 94115
(415) 346-4430
(415) 346-2877 (fax)

Zingerman's
422 Detroit Street
Ann Arbor, MI 48104
(313) 663-3354
(313) 769-1235 (fax)

About the Author

CARLO MIDDIONE has written three other cookbooks, appeared in such widely watched television series as "Carlo Cooks Italian" and the "Tuscan Table," and presided over the instruction of Italian cuisine at the California Culinary Academy. He is also the executive chef and owner of Vivande Ristorante and Vivande Porta Via in San Francisco.